ONE BILLS DRIVE

The Buffalo Bills' GREATEST HOME GAMES 1973–2025

BY GREG D. TRANTER AND BUDD BAILEY

REEDY PRESS

DEDICATIONS

— FROM BUDD —

To my wife Jody, who remains supportive of my literary efforts after more than 35 years—even if she's still hoping that the next book has something to do with her beloved New York Mets.

— FROM GREG —

To my wife Tracy, who continues to be my biggest supporter of all my various sports related research and writing endeavors.

Reedy Press
PO Box 5131
St. Louis, MO 63139, USA
reedypress.com

Library of Congress Control Number: 2025946823

ISBN: 9781681066257

Cover and interior design: Craig Gartner
Front Cover Photograph: Courtesy Getty Images.
Back Cover Photographs: *(left)* Courtesy Getty Images, *(right)* Courtesy Robert L. Smith, Orchard Park, NY.

Printed in Canada
25 26 27 28 29 5 4 3 2 1

CONTENTS

INTRODUCTION

MAN PLANS. And the(football) gods laugh.

The authors were putting the final, final touches on this book when the Bills began the 2025 season with a highly anticipated game with the Baltimore Ravens—the last opening game in the history of what is now Highmark Stadium. Little did they know that the matchup would produce the most exciting regular-season game in the history of One Bills Drive. Buffalo erased a 15-point lead in the final four minutes to win in regulation time by a score of 41-40. It was a first in NFL history. The contest caused some frantic last-minute editing decisions that are now happily in the rear-view mirror.

The Ravens' game proved that the 52-year-old stadium was still capable of hosting memorable contests; it probably will produce more great games in its final weeks. But that doesn't diminish all of the thrills that were provided from August 1973 to January 2025, and that's when the 50 games reviewed on these pages were played.

The road to publication started in 2021, when the members of the Western New York chapter of the Professional Football Researchers Association voted on the greatest home games in the history of the Orchard Park facility. It became a logical jump in 2025 to update that list in a book.

There are many people to thank here. It starts with Reedy Press, which published another book by us in 2023. Owner Josh Stevens, production manager Barbara Northcott, and the rest of the company's staff handled the first book with tender loving care, and it was wonderful to be back with them this time around.

Mike Haim, an expert in all things statistical for Buffalo sports, supplied some information on Bills history. Craig Smith gave us access to the Robert L. Smith photo archives. He was on the Rich Stadium turf from 1973 to 2001 in his role as team photographer. Also, thanks to Kristin Glaspy and the Buffalo History Museum for access to their Buffalo Bills Collection.

In terms of source material, no one writes a book like this without crediting the website Pro Football Reference. The same could be said for newspapers.com, which was invaluable in supplying information and quotes about the games listed. We salute all of the people who covered the Bills over the years, especially from *The Buffalo News*. The authors also accessed several books on the Bills' home games over the years that were extremely helpful.

When the late Ken Dryden was the president of the Toronto Maple Leafs in 1999, he said this about the team's move from Maple Leaf Gardens to the Air Canada Center: "Endings are sad, and beginnings are scary." Bills' fans knew all about that as they prepared to say goodbye to the building at One Bills Drive. But they were packing some great memories—including that Ravens' game, the first to be won by the Bills in Orchard Park on the game's last play in regulation time—as the season counted down. Someday those supporters will look at a parking lot across the street from the "new stadium" and remember that they experienced some of the best moments of their rooting lives on that spot. Hopefully this book will remind you of many of them.

THE STADIUM At ONE BILLS DRIVE

THE BUFFALO BILLS began their professional football journey in 1959 as part of the newly created American Football League. If not for the presence of War Memorial Stadium, owner Ralph C. Wilson Jr. would have placed his franchise in another city. However, now Buffalo had what could be considered a major league team, though nobody was certain if the franchise would still be alive three years later, let alone 66 years.

War Memorial Stadium was a Great Depression–era structure, built on the site of the Prospect Reservoir in Buffalo by the Works Progress Administration. The building, which could hold 36,500 when it opened in 1937, hosted a variety of events, and not just the traditional sports events such as baseball and football. For example, legendary auto race car driver Richard Petty's second NASCAR race was at WMS on July 19, 1958.

War Memorial Stadium was a functional facility for the early years of the team, but the place didn't age particularly well. Somewhere along the way, it picked up the nickname of "The Old Rockpile." Since the stadium was right in the middle of an urban neighborhood, parking was always a problem for events.

Following the June 8, 1966, merger between the AFL and NFL, each franchise was required to have a 50,000-seat stadium by 1970. At that point, if Buffalo was going to be part of the NFL it would need a new facility. Thus began a pot-holed road to a new stadium that eventually ended in Orchard Park, New York.

CREDIT ROBERT L. SMITH, ORCHARD PARK, NY

No less than five different sites were seriously considered by the Erie County Legislature that started as early as February 1963. Following the merger, there was a stipulation in the Bills 1967 lease agreement for the continued use of War Memorial Stadium that a new stadium would be under construction in the third year of the lease (1969). "Nobody can question the gross inadequacy of War Memorial Stadium for major league sports," Wilson said. "It is not of sufficient size for the interest pro football commands. And as our fans are quick to let us know, [it] lacks the ordinary comforts a facility must have to provide for capacity crowds. In short, the future of the Bills cannot be tied to the stadium."

During the next six years, four different sites were considered, one in Amherst, one downtown at the Crossroads (not far from Memorial Auditorium) a site in Lancaster (a domed stadium), and at the fairgrounds in Hamburg. All met serious resistance for one reason or another. In the meantime, Wilson had little choice but to begin to look elsewhere. He had serious discussions with the city of Seattle where voters had approved a $40 million multi-purpose domed stadium, and the threat of Buffalo losing the Bills was very real.

Finally in March 1971 after the fairgrounds site was spurned, the county pivoted and decided to utilize land in Orchard Park that was already owned by the county. The county allotted 20 acres that had been reserved for the future South Towns Community College project that could be carved out separately. A triangle shaped area was identified for the stadium—the space bounded by Southwestern Boulevard, Abbott Road, and Big Tree Road.

The new site was approved by the Erie County Legislature, which also approved a $20.5 million bond issue on June 22. The Bills and Erie County agreed to a 25-year lease for an 80,000-seat facility, and the deal was signed on October 15. The timetable for the new stadium was for the commencement of construction in April 1972 with completion in July 1973.

"Personally, I couldn't be happier. I came to Buffalo in 1959 and agreed to put together a professional football team on the basis of a handshake," the Bills' owner said. "Now I know I will spend the rest of my life as part of that tradition."

The stadium construction bids were received by Erie County and were opened on March 24, 1972. The outcome to the delight of Erie County Legislature chairman Richard J. Keane was the bids came in below the amount appropriated for the construction. In total, they were under $19 million. "I am overjoyed and very, very happy," Keane said. The legislature awarded contracts to the lowest bidders on March 27. The John W. Cowper Co., Inc. of Buffalo was selected as the General Contractor with a bid of $15,722,389.71. Separate awards were also given for plumbing, heating and ventilating, and electrical work.

The moment all Buffalo football fans had been hoping and waiting for finally arrived on April 4, when ground was officially broken for a new football stadium with a dynamite blast. A journey of more than six years had led to the start of construction. The first shovel of dirt was turned jointly by Keane and Wilson with more than 350 onlookers. A band played "Happy Days are Here Again." "This is a beautiful day for Erie County, a beautiful day for Buffalo and a beautiful day for Orchard Park," Wilson said.

With construction underway, the legislature decided to explore the possibility of selling the naming rights to a private company for the stadium. Naming a stadium after a private company was almost unheard of at that time. This would lead to another harangue and a lawsuit that would take several years to solve. Rich Products Corp. originally offered $1 million over 10 years for the right to name the facility "Coffee Rich Park." Wilson called that "crass

The Stadium groundbreaking on April 4, 1972
CREDIT ROBERT L. SMITH, ORCHARD PARK, NY

commercialism." Eventually, Rich Products was awarded the naming rights for 25 years at a cost of $1.5 million, and the facility would carry the name of Rich Stadium. The Bills were totally opposed to a commercial name to the stadium and offered several alternatives, to no avail. The team refused to use the name until lawsuits were filed and eventually Wilson and Bob Rich Sr. solved the disagreement several years later.

The Bills increased ticket prices with the opening of the new stadium. The prices went up by $1 or $1.50 to $5.50, $7.00, and $8.50 per game. With the anticipation of the new stadium, despite the price increases, the Bills sold the 46,207th season ticket on March 29, and that sale assured the team would have their largest home crowds ever for the 1973 season.

Rich Stadium, with its gleaming green astroturf field, officially opened on August 17 with the Bills hosting the Washington Redskins in front of a sellout crowd of 80,020. "This place is beautiful," Perry Kays from Pittsford said. "The seats we have on the 10-yard line here are better than the 40-yard line at old War Memorial Stadium," Buffalonian John Bondi said. "There aren't any obstacles. There's more leg room here, and everything is cleaner."

The completion of the stadium enabled Buffalo to truly become a major league sports city. Its sports future was secure. Buffalo was in the NFL to stay.

"The team was committed to Buffalo," Wilson said years later. "I never had any idea of not getting the best for Buffalo. The league said, 'Hey, the stadium downtown is too small, you need at least 50,000 seats,' so in order to stay in the league, we had to get a new stadium."

The football-designed stadium paid off right away for the Bills. With the best sightlines in the NFL, the team not only set franchise attendance records, but also league records. The Bills drew 531,270 people in 1973 to set an NFL stadium attendance record. They led the league again in 1974 and 1975.

After the stadium's original construction, the facility underwent many improvements. With some of those improvements adding capacity, the Bills led the NFL in attendance for six consecutive seasons from 1988–1993 and broke the single season NFL attendance record in 1991 when they drew 635,889, despite playing in the second-smallest market in the league.

On March 28, 2022, the Bills, Erie County, and New York State reached an agreement for a 62,000-seat, $1.4 billion dollar stadium to be built in Orchard Park directly across the street from Highmark Stadium. With its opening in 2026, the last NFL regular-season game played at the old facility will be on January 4, 2026, against the New York Jets.

PRESEASON

AUGUST 17, 1973

REDSKINS At BILLS

THIS IS the only preseason game listed in this book of great moments at One Bills Drive. The score has been forgotten by almost everyone. Only one play—the first one—comes to mind when recalling the game itself. Yet those who were there will never forget the day the Bills opened their new stadium.

It is important to remember what the team's situation was before this game. The Bills arrived in 1960 as a member of the new American Football League. They played their games in War Memorial Stadium, a structure built in 1937 that had decayed over the years. But the aging facility fulfilled the promise for what the team needed when it first arrived, and would leave no doubt that Buffalo would be a big league city. The Bills had some good memories there, including two championship teams. But a better, more modern facility was needed.

Finally, in 1973, the team had a new home. It was located in Orchard Park, and was everything the old place wasn't—new and big. It was "big league" and all that entailed.

"I'll never forget War Memorial Stadium," Mark Holdren of Honeoye Falls told the *Rochester Democrat & Chronicle*. "The place was unique. Not nice—unique. I wouldn't want to go back to it, but I'd like one brick to remember it by."

There are still some old-timers around who remember that first game, and their biggest memory of the night comes in the form of one of the great traffic jams in Western New York history. The Bills had 80,020 people coming to the game, and most of them had little idea on where to park. Throw in the fact that the Erie County Fair was opening on its grounds a mile away, and you had the makings of gridlock. Authorities had never worked with this size of a crowd, and they needed some practice to figure out what procedures were necessary to improve the traffic flow. As a result, some fans were very

John Mosier caught the first Bills' touchdown pass in Rick Stadium's history.

CREDIT ROBERT L. SMITH, ORCHARD PARK, NY

late in arriving, with a handful turning up in the fourth quarter.

Some fans must have wondered if the move was a good idea, if only for a moment.

Imagine the excitement, however, when the game actually started—at least for those in the building. Buffalo's John Leypoldt kicked the ball into the end zone. Herb Mul-Key of the Redskins caught it, and came charging up field. Mul-Key kept running through the Bills' return team and down the field, and he didn't stop until he had covered 102 yards. It took him 15 seconds. It was memorable if not particularly appreciated.

"What did I see?" Mul-Key said in response to a question. "I didn't see nobody. Just a big hole and I went through it."

Washington also had the first field goal in Rich Stadium history (Curt Knight), and the first touchdown pass in Rich Stadium history (Billy Kilmer to Charlie Taylor). Joe Ferguson, the Bills' third-round draft choice from Arkansas, had the first three Bills' touchdown passes in the new digs. Ferguson was probably the biggest story of the night. He was scheduled to split duty in the game with veteran Dennis Shaw, but the rookie played well enough to play the entire game. On this night, Ferguson earned the chance to continue to battle for the starting job.

"I think he showed a lot of stuff in stepping away from the rush," Bills coach Lou Saban said. "He never got rattled and he threw well."

Then it was time to go home . . . eventually. The parking lots at Rich Stadium weren't empty until 1 a.m.

"I think it's a beautiful stadium," George Allen, Washington's head coach, said. "It's one of the nicer stadiums I've been in."

From the team's perspective, the opener was another checkmark on the way to the regular season opener. The Bills had lost their first three preseason games, and time was counting down before the start of the regular season. "We've got a pretty good idea of who's going to be able to play," Saban said. "Sure, we've got a long way to go, a lot of things to do. We know what has to be done."

On the other hand, the opening of the stadium ensured that the Bills would have a place in the NFL for years to come.

Ranked No. 19 of 50 by the authors.

BOX SCORE

	1ST	2ND	3RD	4TH	FINAL
WASHINGTON (W)	17	14	3	3	37
BUFFALO (L)	0	14	0	7	21

SCORING SUMMARY:

QTR	TEAM	PLAY
1ST	WAS.	Mul-Key 102-yard kickoff return (Knight kick)
1ST	WAS.	Knight 14-yard field goal
1ST	WAS.	Kilmer 22-yard pass to Taylor (Knight kick)
2ND	BUF.	Ferguson 10-yard pass to Mosier (Leypoldt kick)
2ND	WAS.	Harraway 2-yard run (Knight kick)
2ND	WAS.	Thomas 1-yard run (Knight kick)
2ND	BUF.	Ferguson 55-yard pass to Hill (Clark kick)
3RD	WAS.	Knight 16-yard field goal
4TH	WAS.	Knight 42-yard field goal
4TH	BUF.	Ferguson 18-yard pass to Harrison (Leypoldt kick)

ATTENDANCE: 80,020

NOTEWORTHY: *Ferguson was 18 of 32 for 171 yards. A moment of silence was held before the game in memory of Bob Kalsu, a Bills lineman who was killed in Vietnam. The crowd was announced as 80,020, which would mean there weren't any no-shows. That seems rather unlikely, as there certainly must have been a few people who became fed up with the traffic and went home. Still, the number stood. Fans received a special coin when they walked in the door that read, "I was there."*

ONE BILLS DRIVE

OCTOBER 29, 1973

CHIEFS At BILLS

FOR THOSE who weren't around in the early 1970s, it's difficult to understand how big Monday Night Football was at that time.

The National Football League had started playing one night game a week in 1970, and some wondered if a game in prime time would attract the attention of America. ABC won the bidding rights, and hired Keith Jackson (replaced a year later by Frank Gifford), Howard Cosell, and Don Meredith as the commentators. The games were an almost instant smash, as sports fans all over the country changed their life's routines on Monday night to watch.

The only catch from a Western New York standpoint was that Buffalo had not hosted a Monday night game in the first three years of the broadcast, so it missed out on the fun. Part of the problem was that the Bills were quite terrible during that era, and part of that was no one was too anxious to present crumbling War Memorial Stadium as the face of Buffalo to the nation.

But in 1973, much had changed. The Bills had a new playpen called Rich Stadium, which had been a big hit in the first half of the season. The NFL scheduled a home game for them against the Kansas City Chiefs.

The lights are a little brighter in prime time, and every television production needs a star that can attract viewers. This presentation of Monday Night Football had that with the presence of O.J. Simpson. He had become the biggest name in the sport after running for 868 yards through six games, even though he was kept under 100 for the first time that season by Miami a week before this game. As the season reached its midway point, every football fan in Western New York did the math. O.J. only needed 132 yards in the seventh game to reach the magical 1,000-yard mark.

And if he could do that in the first half of the season, why couldn't he do it again in the second half of the season to reach the seemingly impossible number of 2,000 yards rushing for the year?

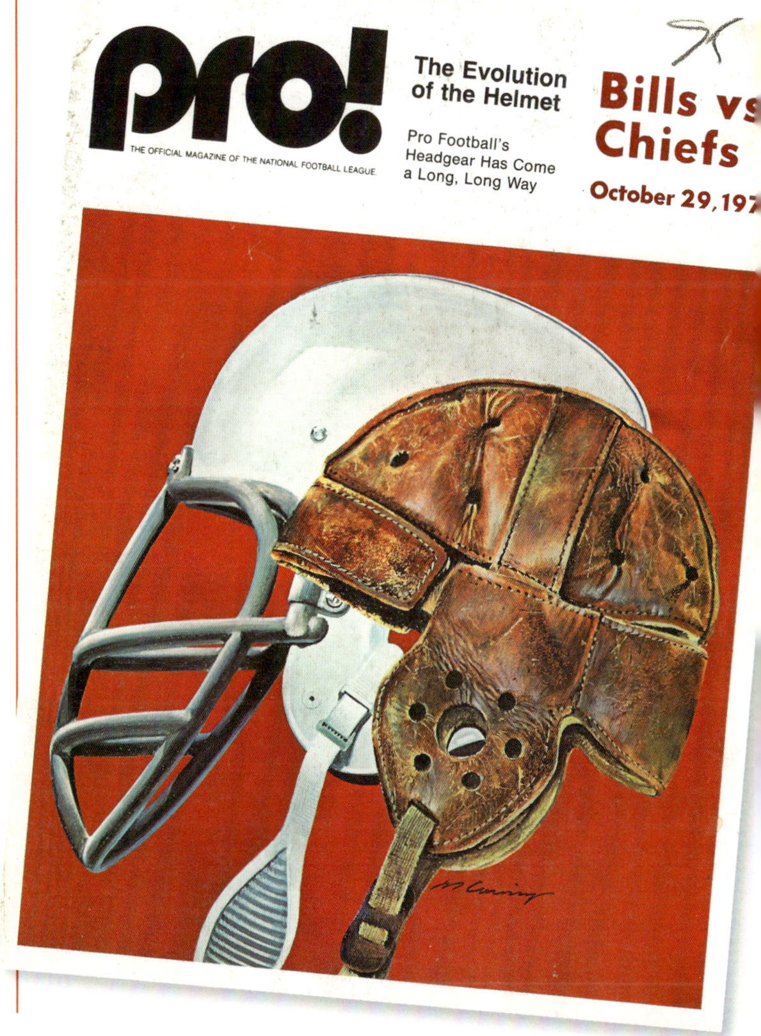

If America wanted to see Simpson, the Bills were happy to oblige . . . and then some.

Buffalo set the tone right away. Kansas City fumbled the ball on its second play, and Jim Cheyunski recovered for the Bills on the Chiefs' 15. It took four straight runs for Simpson to score, but his 1-yard run gave Buffalo the early lead. Later in the first quarter, it was the same story. Cheyunski intercepted Len Dawson's pass and returned it 31 yards to the KC four-yard line. Simpson immediately ran it in for another touchdown to make it 14–0.

"Any time you're playing a squad that is in an emotional frenzy like Buffalo was—and motivated by their fans—and you give two touchdowns away right off the bat, you're in trouble," Chiefs coach Hank Stram said.

This was not a night for the Bills to stage any sensational plays, as their longest gain was a 22-yard run by Simpson. But there was no denying the effectiveness of the offense. The Chiefs cut the lead in half on the only score in the second quarter, which probably convinced a few million viewers to hang around for the second half. They saw John Leypoldt kick three field goals to make it a 23–7 lead.

The Buffalo defense certainly deserved some credit for the way the game was headed. The coaching

O.J Simpson cracked the 1,000-yard mark for the season in a win against the Chiefs.
CREDIT ROBERT L. SMITH, ORCHARD PARK, NY

staff substituted a linebacker for a safety, catching the Chiefs unprepared. "If their blocking is jammed up, it shuts off their running game," Cheyunski said. "But the defense was also effective against their passing. Playing with only one safety is a hazard, but we were getting such a strong pass rush that their quarterbacks couldn't take advantage."

In the fourth quarter, the only score came on Pete Beathard's touchdown run for the Chiefs. But the 23–14 lead held, as Simpson and Larry Watkins chewed up the clock in the final minutes with effective ball-control runs.

"We needed this victory because we needed to prove we could do it to a good team," Bills head coach Lou Saban said.

BOX SCORE

	1ST	2ND	3RD	4TH	FINAL
KANSAS CITY (L, 3-3-1)	0	0	7	7	14
BUFFALO (W, 5-2)	14	0	9	0	23

SCORING SUMMARY:

QTR	TEAM	PLAY
1ST	BUF.	Simpson 1-yard run (Leypoldt kick)
1ST	BUF.	Simpson 4-yard run (Chandler run)
2nd	K.C.	Hayes 1-yard run (Stenerud kick)
3RD	BUF.	Leypoldt 31-yard field goal
3RD	BUF.	Leypoldt 17-yard field goal
3RD	BUF.	Leypoldt 8-yard field goal
4TH	K.C.	Beathard 2-yard run (Stenerud kick)

ATTENDANCE: 76,071

When the game was over, Simpson had run for 157 yards on the night, putting him over the thousand mark (1,025). No one had done that in seven games, and a 2,000-yard season definitely was in play. "We got 1,000 in the first seven games and we'll go for another 1,000 yards in the next seven," Simpson said.

What's more, O.J. had 39 carries to set an NFL record. "I didn't realize I carried the ball that much because I wasn't getting tired," Simpson said. "I was getting cramps in my legs. Our running game will get better as [quarterback Joe] Ferguson matures."

It added up to a Monday night to remember.

Ranked No. 38 of 50 by the authors.

NOTEWORTHY: *The Bills' defense held Kansas City to eight first downs and 38 yards rushing. Buffalo also finished with four sacks. Joe Ferguson almost could have played the game in a rocking chair, since he threw only 11 passes. Six of them were caught—three by Bob Chandler and three by J.D. Hill. The Bills' fifth win of the season meant they already had won more games in 1973 than they did in all of 1972. The game was blacked out in Buffalo, as 1,478 tickets had not been purchased at the 72-hour deadline.*

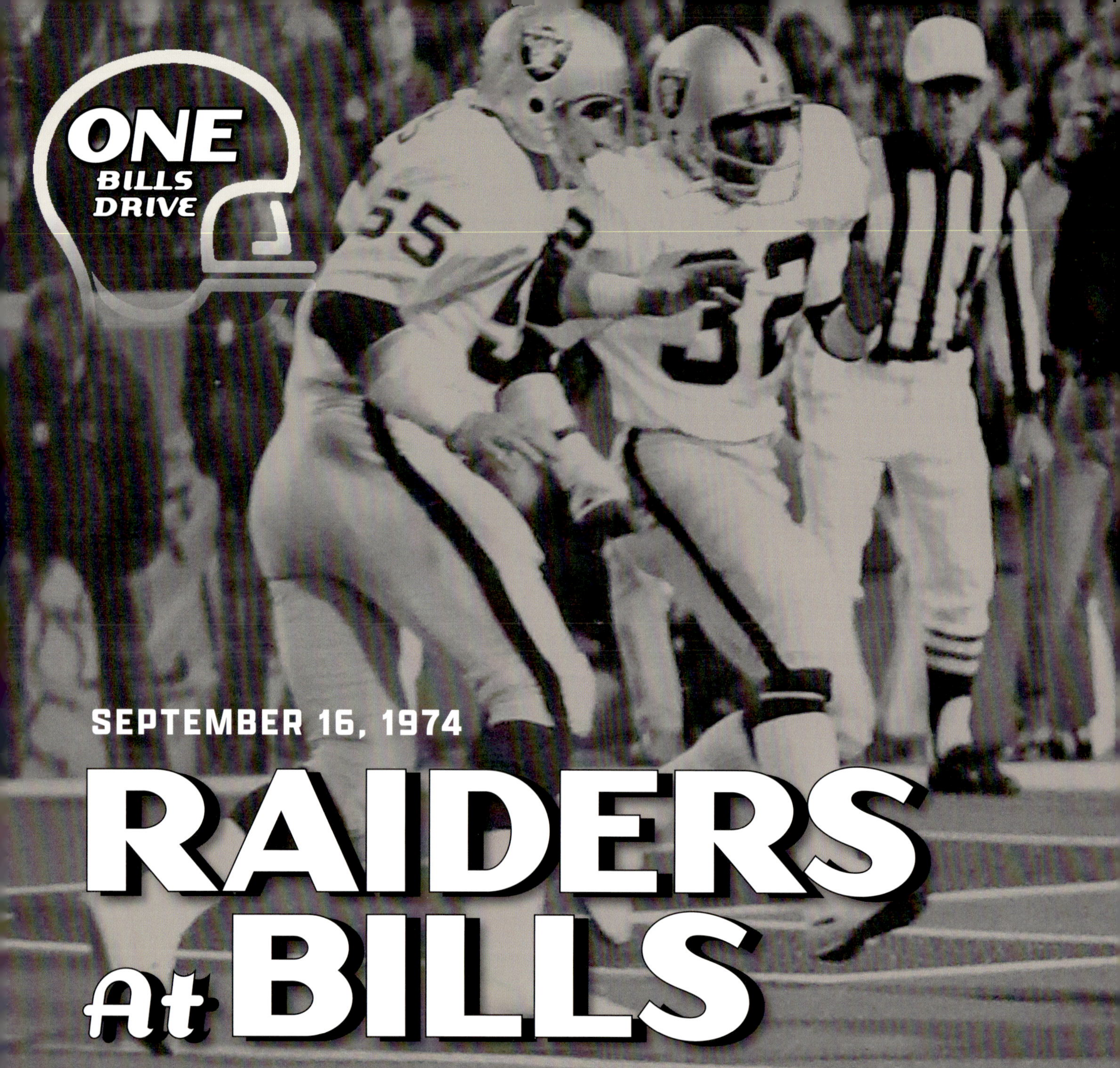

SEPTEMBER 16, 1974

RAIDERS At BILLS

OPENING DAY of the 1974 NFL season figured to be one to remember for the Bills.

Buffalo was coming off its best season since formally joining the NFL in 1970 and its first winning season since 1966. Bills fans couldn't wait to see what the encore season might look like.

The NFL schedule-maker provided an extra boost for Buffalo's opener. Not only would the Bills go up against the Oakland Raiders, one of the perennial powerhouses of the league, but the game also would be shown on Monday Night Football.

While the Bills still figured to rely on Simpson in 1974, their offense was expected to be more balanced than it had been the year before. Joe Ferguson was now in his second year starting at quarterback, and Ahmad Rashad had been added to a wide receiver group that already had J.D. Hill and Bob Chandler.

"We may pass more, but not that much more," Ferguson said before the season. "O.J.

Ahmad Rashad's two late touchdown catches lifted the Bills to victory in their 1974 opener.
CREDIT ROBERT L. SMITH, ORCHARD PARK, NY

may run a little less, but instead of averaging six yards a carry, he may get 20."

A sellout crowd at Rich Stadium watched a game that featured a huge plot twist, so to speak, and the most two-sided ending in franchise history.

The Bills' first good drive of the game started with 10 consecutive handoffs, seven to Simpson, that gained 47 yards. Ferguson then crossed up Oakland by actually throwing a pass, his first attempt of the game, to a wide-open Hill in the end zone.

Late in the half, the Raiders' George Blanda converted a short field goal. Less than a minute later, Ferguson had moved the Bills to the Oakland 30-yard line, but John Leypoldt missed the 37-yard field goal attempt.

The twist in the story came in that drive when Simpson sprained his ankle during a 20-yard run and was out for the rest of the game.

"I was trying to take it all the way," Simpson said. "I cut to the right and saw [cornerback Skip] Thomas in front of me, so I tried to take it back all the way to the left. When I made my cut, I could feel my ankle twist and I just sort of fell into his arms."

Oakland came out with a vengeance to begin the second half. Davis swept around left end for a 15-yard touchdown to put the Raiders in the lead. That was soon followed by another field goal by Blanda to put Oakland up 13–7.

With two minutes left in the game the Bills had the ball on fourth down at the Oakland eight-yard line. "I just told our linemen in the huddle, 'You know what we have to do. They know what we have to do. So, I'm asking you for a little extra time,'" Ferguson said. The Bills' quarterback threw an 8-yard pass to Rashad for a touchdown. Leypoldt's extra point gave the Bills a 14–13 lead.

But Buffalo could not stand prosperity. The Bills' defense stopped the Raiders on three plays and forced a punt. Victory seemed almost assured. Then disaster struck. On the first play following the punt, Jim Braxton fumbled, and Raiders defensive tackle Art Thoms picked up the loose ball and ran 29 yards for the score, putting the Raiders in the lead 20–14. "My heart sank," Simpson said, "when I saw Art Thoms pick up that fumble and start to run."

There was still 1:08 remaining, so the Bills had a chance. Ferguson completed three passes, and the Bills were helped by two Oakland penalties to put the ball on the Raiders' 13 with 35 seconds left. Ferguson threw a 13-yard touchdown pass to Rashad, who caught the pass while falling into the end zone. "When you get inside their 30, they almost have to give you single coverage," Rashad said. "I just don't think anyone is going to cover me one on one."

The score prompted the third celebration by either team in the final two minutes. Yet there were still 31 seconds left. In two plays, Stabler moved the Raiders to Buffalo's 33-yard line. On the final play of the game, Blanda missed a 50-yard field goal attempt and the Bills were victorious—prompting the fourth and final celebration, the biggest of them all.

"On that last drive we knew Joe could take us in if we kept everybody off him," Bills' center Mike Montler said. "We just had our tails nailed to the ground. Oakland is always physical and they try to intimidate you, get you to worry about your health."

In the process, the Bills showed that they were not a one-man team—and might be a factor in the playoff race in 1974.

"When Juice went down it was a blow," Bills' guard Reggie McKenzie said. "When they made the touchdown on the fumble it was a blow. But we came back. We showed 'em something. They call it 'character' and 'class.'"

Ranked No. 4 of 50 by the authors.

BOX SCORE

	1ST	2ND	3RD	4TH	FINAL
OAKLAND (L, 0-1)	0	3	7	10	20
BUFFALO (W, 1-0)	0	7	0	14	21

SCORING SUMMARY:

QTR	TEAM	PLAY
2ND	BUF.	Ferguson 4-yard pass to Hill (Leypoldt kick)
2ND	OAK.	Blanda 34-yard field goal
3RD	OAK.	Davis 15-yard run (Blanda kick)
4TH	OAK.	Blanda 41-yard field goal
4TH	BUF.	Ferguson 8-yard pass to Rashad (Leypoldt kick)
4TH	OAK.	Thoms 29-yard fumble return (Blanda kick)
4TH	BUF.	Ferguson 13-yard pass to Rashad (Leypoldt kick)

ATTENDANCE: 79,876

NOTEWORTHY: *Buffalo rushed for 200 yards on 45 carries led by Simpson's 78 yards and Braxton with 69. Ferguson completed 10 of 20 passes for 122 yards and three touchdowns. The Bills defense held Stabler to 100 yards passing on 9 of 22. Buffalo outgained Oakland 306 to 252.*

SEPTEMBER 29, 1974

JETS At BILLS

WHEN TEAMS come to Buffalo to play at Rich Stadium they somewhat expect to run into unpredictable weather, especially late in the season. But the New York Jets certainly did not expect the terrible conditions for a game played in late September that they experienced on this day.

The game was played in a chilling, driving rain and 40 mile-per-hour winds that left both quarterbacks very ineffective in throwing the football. "The wind was bad, but we had rain coming down so hard. And it was not dropping straight out of the sky," Bills quarterback Joe Ferguson said. "It was coming down at an angle and hitting you in the eye."

After the game, Jets quarterback Joe Namath said, "The weather, the rain and the big wind, was ridiculous. The conditions were so bad that if it had been a golf tournament—instead of a football game—they'd have called it off. I don't recall ever trying to throw under worse conditions."

William N. Wallace of the *New York Times* put it this way: "The goal posts wobbled. Center snaps for punts and placekicks went awry. Punts were great downwind, terrible upwind. The ball had to be held on kickoffs. A new American flag became frayed at its ends."

With the weather conditions, the Bills took advantage of their backfield duo of O.J. Simpson and Jim Braxton. In the first quarter Buffalo ran the ball 16 times for 73 yards and scored the first touchdown on a 1-yard sneak by Ferguson. The touchdown was set up by a Tony Greene interception and a return of 20 yards to the Jets' 5-yard line. The Namath pass was knocked down by the gale force winds with the ball falling well short of his intended receiver and Greene snagged the errant throw.

The Bills relied on runs from players such as Jim Braxton on a miserable day for football.

CREDIT ROBERT L. SMITH, ORCHARD PARK, NY

O.J. Simpson was one of the few players who could navigate through a rainstorm on a miserable day for football.

CREDIT ROBERT L. SMITH, ORCHARD PARK, NY

The Bills added a John Leypoldt 21-yard field goal in the second quarter following a 15-play, 88-yard drive—all running plays. The Jets scored their only touchdown midway through the second quarter, following Braxton's fumble on the Buffalo 25-yard line. The extra point failed due to a wind-blown snap from center, and the Jets trailed 10–6.

At halftime, Ferguson was officially 0 for 1 passing, but had two other passes intercepted that were both nullified by penalty. Namath had attempted seven passes with no completions and one interception. Meanwhile, Bills' rookie offensive lineman Joe DeLamielleure had to change part of his equipment in the middle of the game.

"I wrecked a pair of shoes that day," he wrote in a memoir later. "I was so cold that I kept sticking my feet into the hot-air blower, and I melted my cleats off. I tried playing in them, even with the cleats melted off, but I couldn't get any traction, and I had to change shoes mid-game."

In the third quarter, New York took advantage of good field position twice, aided by the wind, to score two field goals. Only three passes were thrown in the third quarter and all fell incomplete as both teams had acquiesced to the weather. "We just said the devil with it and stuck with our running game," Bills coach Lou Saban said. "You won't ever find conditions any worse than today." No passes had been completed by either team through three quarters.

On the Bills' second possession of the fourth quarter, they took over on the 50-yard line following a 26-yard punt into the gusty wind. Buffalo ran the ball down the Jets' throat on the drive. Simpson carried five times for 21 yards, and Braxton ran three times for 29 yards, including a 21-yard touchdown jaunt to give his team the lead.

With the Jets trying to play catch-up and less than two minutes remaining, the first pass of the game finally was completed. Namath fired a 12-yard swing pass to David Knight. The Jets quarterback completed one other pass on the day, but that would be it. After a few more incompletions, Namath threw a windblown pass that was intercepted by Robert James.

The Jets had one final chance after stopping the Bills and forcing a punt. But linebacker Rich Lewis intercepted the Jets quarterback with 17 seconds left to secure the victory for Buffalo.

Ranked No. 47 of 50 by the authors.

BOX SCORE

	1ST	2ND	3RD	4TH	FINAL
N.Y. JETS (L, 1-1)	0	6	6	0	12
BUFFALO (W, 1-1)	7	3	0	6	16

SCORING SUMMARY:

QTR	TEAM	PLAY
1ST	BUF.	Ferguson 1-yard run (Leypoldt kick)
2ND	BUF.	Leypoldt 21-yard field goal
2ND	NYJ.	Riggins 13-yard run (kick failed)
3RD	NYJ.	Howfield 31-yard field goal
3RD	NYJ.	Howfield 40-yard field goal
4TH	BUF.	Braxton 21-yard run (kick failed)

ATTENDANCE: 76,978

NOTEWORTHY: *It was the worst game of Namath's career, at least in terms of passing percentage. He was 2 of 18, an 11.1 percent completion rate, for 33 yards and three interceptions. In other words, he completed more passes to the Bills than to the Jets. Buffalo rushed for 223 yards on 61 carries while the Jets netted only 106 yards rushing on 33 tries. Simpson led all rushers with 117 yards on 31 attempts; it was his first 100-yard game of the season. Braxton chipped in with 84 yards on 17 carries. Ferguson finished the game 0 for 2 passing with zero yards. The Bills became the first team in the Super Bowl era to win a game without completing a pass. What's more, they still are the only team that has won in that manner. Only 3,042 did not use their tickets on a miserable day for watching football.*

Buffalo quarterback Joe Ferguson and tackle Donnie Green were left discouraged by yet another loss to the Dolphins.
CREDIT ROBERT L. SMITH, ORCHARD PARK, NY

OCTOBER 26, 1975

DOLPHINS At BILLS

THE BILLS went winless in the decade of the 1970s in regular-season games against the Miami Dolphins, a record that will never be broken under the current scheduling format. Not all of those games were one-sided, of course, with some of the close contests played in Buffalo's home. In a book like this, it's necessary to have a representative game listed, as the streak is an important if frustrating part of Bills history.

In 1978, Buffalo dropped a 25–24 decision at Rich Stadium, and a year later, the Dolphins went home with a 9–7 victory. But for pure agony, the 1975 matchup represents the closest call of the decade. After all, it looked like the Bills were about to break through . . . but didn't.

The first point to remember about the game was that it was a good matchup. Both teams came into the contest at 4–1, tied atop the AFC East. The Bills had opened the season with four straight wins, averaging 37 points per game in the process. The team was coming off a playoff appearance in 1974, its first since 1966. The Bills had O.J. Simpson at the peak of his powers and a maturing Joe Ferguson at quarterback. But the Dolphins were still good, as usual. They were in the midst of a run that saw them win at least 10 games in the regular season for the previous five years. That's even more impressive in an era of a 14-game schedule.

When the teams did get to work on this particular day, they put on quite a show. Larry Felser, reporter for *The Buffalo Evening News*, put it this way: "It was the type of football game Pete Rozelle, the National (Football) League commissioner, prays that every Super Bowl will be, but never is."

If Buffalo needed a good start to boost its confidence, it certainly received one in the first quarter. Steve Freeman intercepted Bob Griese's overthrown pass and waltzed into the end zone. When Simpson later ran for a score, the Bills had a 13–0 lead before the end of the period.

The teams went back and forth for the rest of the game. The Dolphins clawed back within striking distance, and the Bills answered with a score of their own. Ferguson had a couple of touchdown passes to Bob Chandler along the way. The second of those passes gave the Bills a 30–21 lead with seven minutes to go. A win over the Dolphins was almost close enough to taste.

But Miami wasn't done. After a methodical and efficient drive, Griese threw to tight end Jim Mandich for a touchdown to cut the Bills' lead to 30–28. Then came the play of the game. Buffalo had the ball on its own 12-yard line with a little more than three minutes to go. Simpson—the game's best running back—was ready to pick up some yards in chunks and kill the clock.

Instead, the Bills opted to try a first-down pass. Ferguson's pass to J.D. Hill was tipped at the line of scrimmage and intercepted by safety Jake Scott, and the Dolphins were in business at the Buffalo 22. "I think Scott read the play," Hill said. "I made my move and the ball was there, but so was he."

Ferguson might have been confused by the fact that Miami switched into a zone defense for one of the few times in the game. "Sure, it was gutsy," Scott said about the call. "But the kid had been doing so well and he needed the yards. If they don't get a first down and have to punt from there, we're going to come back and kick a field goal and win, anyway."

Six plays later, Nottingham ran the ball in from 1 yard out with about 90 seconds left. The Bills had one last drive in an attempt to win the game, and reached the Miami 38. Then Ferguson fumbled, Vern Den Herder of the Dolphins recovered, and Miami finished with a 35–30 win.

BOX SCORE

	1ST	2ND	3RD	4TH	FINAL
MIAMI (W, 5-1)	0	14	7	14	35
BUFFALO (L, 4-2)	13	10	0	7	30

SCORING SUMMARY:

QTR	TEAM	PLAY
1ST	BUF.	Freeman 30-yard interception return (Leypoldt kick)
1ST	BUF.	Simpson 26-yard run (kick failed)
2ND	MIA.	Nottingham 1-yard run (Yepremian kick)
2ND	BUF.	Ferguson 4-yard pass to Chandler (Leypoldt kick)
2ND	MIA	Griese 13-yard pass to Moore (Yepremian kick)
2ND	BUF.	Leypoldt 45-yard field goal
3RD	MIA.	Nottingham 1-yard run (Yepremian kick)
4TH	BUF.	Ferguson 5-yard pass to Chandler (Leypoldt kick)
4TH	MIA.	Griese 5-yard pass to Mandich (Yepremian kick)
4TH	MIA.	Nottingham 1-yard run (Yepremian kick)

ATTENDANCE: 79,141

The Dolphins were left relieved and happy. "It was as big a victory for this team as our two Super Bowl wins," Miami guard Bob Kuechenberg slightly overstated in the thrill of victory.

And you can imagine how well this one went over in the Buffalo locker room. "It was brutal, just brutal," Bills coach Lou Saban said. "We played so well. But it wasn't good enough. One costly mistake."

Ranked No. 25 of 50 by the authors.

NOTEWORTHY: *The Dolphins pounded out 229 yards rushing in the game, with Mercury Morris earning 124 of them. For the Bills, Simpson had 19 runs for 88 yards, his lowest output to that point in the season. It was the seventh straight time that the Dolphins had held Simpson under 100 yards rushing. Ferguson was 20 (then a career high) of 29 for 221 yards, but threw two interceptions. The Bills also lost two fumbles. This was Freeman's first start in the NFL. He played through 1987, and then had a second career as an NFL official.*

SEPTEMBER 9, 1979

BENGALS At BILLS

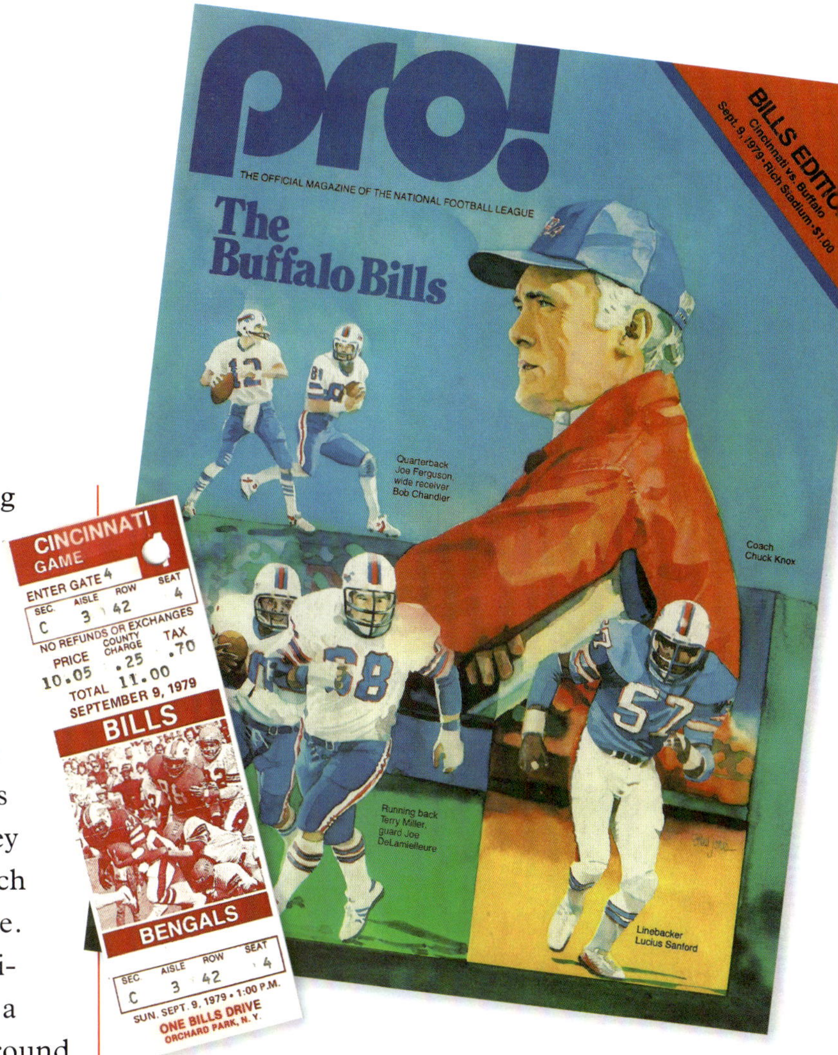

ROLAND HOOKS was something of an unlikely candidate to be a folk hero.

He came out of North Carolina State as one of four running backs on the Wolfpack roster in his sophomore year to play pro football; they were called "The Four Stallions." The others were Stan Fritts, Willie Burden, and Charley Young. That's almost like having too much talent at one position, if that's possible. Hooks helped N.C. State win the ACC title as a junior, and ran for 850 yards as a senior. The Bills took Hooks in the 10th round of the 1975 NFL Draft.

Hooks missed the 1975 season because of illness. Then he made the team's roster in 1976 and hung around for seven seasons. In fact, by 1979 the halfback was the only draftee of the Bills from 1975 who was still on the team's roster. Roland played on some bad teams and some good teams, but he had the knack of contributing in a limited role. Not only did that make him valuable to the Bills, but it also made him popular to the fans.

That leads us to the 1979 game with the Cincinnati Bengals. The Bills were coming off another discouraging loss to the Miami Dolphins in the opener, and expectations were still low as coach Chuck Knox was trying to rebuild the roster. Maybe the visiting Bengals were a good opponent under the circumstances, since they were coming off a 4–12 season.

It took a while for some excitement to arrive. The first quarter was scoreless, and the two teams split 20 points in the second quarter on short plunges and easy field goals.

Then the second half started, and mayhem began. Hooks started it with a short scoring run, dramatically taking out a security guard who was standing near the end zone after the touchdown. The play was followed by a pick-six by Bills' linebacker Isiah Robertson. Even a 73-yard touchdown bomb by the Bengals couldn't slow Buffalo's momentum, because Hooks was still on the job. He ran it in from 32 yards, and the Bills had a 31–17 lead after three quarters.

"It's not easy to make solo tackles like that out in the open when the back can go left, right, or straight through you," Bengals safety Scott Perry

BOX SCORE

	1ST	2ND	3RD	4TH	FINAL
CINCINNATI (L, 0-2)	0	10	7	7	24
BUFFALO (W, 1-1)	0	10	21	20	51

SCORING SUMMARY:

QTR	TEAM	PLAY
2ND	BUF.	Dempsey 18-yard field goal
2ND	CINN.	Johnson 1-yard run (Bahr kick)
2ND	BUF.	Miller 2-yard run (Dempsey kick)
2ND	CINN.	Bahr 24-yard field goal
3RD	BUF.	Hooks 3-yard run (Dempsey kick)
3RD	BUF.	Robertson 23-yard interception return (Dempsey kick)
3RD	CINN.	Anderson 73-yard pass to Brooks (Bahr kick)
3RD	BUF.	Hooks 32-yard run (Dempsey kick)
4TH	BUF.	Hooks 4-yard run (Dempsey kick)
4TH	BUF.	Hooks 28-yard run (kick blocked)
4TH	BUF.	Sanford 3-yard blocked punt return (Dempsey kick)
4TH	CINN.	Thompson 5-yard run (Bahr kick)

ATTENDANCE: 43,504

said. "He [Hooks] just came rolling through there and we didn't have any pursuit."

But Hooks wasn't done. He ran for four yards for another score, and then went 28 yards for yet another touchdown. The latter play saw him come out of a pile at the line of scrimmage, break some tackles, and sprint into the end zone. Cincinnati defender Louis Breeden threw Hooks to the ground after the score, aggravating a back injury by the Buffalo runner. Still, Hooks had done enough for one day.

The halfback had scored four touchdowns in less than a half. Then someone checked the play-by-play sheet, and came to the realization that Hooks had scored touchdowns on four straight carries. That might happen in a high school game occasionally, but it's ridiculous to expect in the pros.

"I knew he was a good running back, but I didn't know he could make some of the moves he made today," quarterback Joe Ferguson said. "I've never seen some moves like that. . . . I've seen O.J. make great moves and great runs, but he and Hooks are different kinds of runners."

Just to add to the fun, the Bills blocked a punt, and Lucius Sanford ran it in for one last score. Cincinnati scored a meaningless touchdown to finish the scoring at 51–24. It was Buffalo's best offensive output in 13 years, since the team ran up 58 points against the first-year Miami Dolphins in 1966.

Hooks finished the game with five runs for 70 yards and the four touchdowns, and he caught three passes for 60 yards—including a 42-yarder.

Roland Hooks had the game of his life in leading the Bills past the Bengals.
CREDIT ROBERT L. SMITH, ORCHARD PARK, NY

"That was a game that I could do very little wrong," Hooks said later to author Jim Gelman. "It's kind of like being in a zone, whatever that is. That game, I guess I kind of was in the zone. For some reason I made people miss. I remember looking at game films, and things seemed to be in slow motion when I was playing. I didn't remember doing some of the things that I had done. . . . It was just a day to remember. It was just an unbelievable day."

Ranked No. 37 of 50 by the authors.

NOTEWORTHY: *Ferguson was right on target throughout the game. The Bills' quarterback was 16 of 21 for 282 yards. Jerry Butler caught seven passes for 116 yards. Buffalo finished with 209 yards rushing. At the time, it was the worst defeat in the history of the Bengals.*

BORO

SEPTEMBER 23, 1979

JETS At BILLS

NOT TOO MANY football players could be described as "elegant" in their playing style. Jerry Butler was an exception.

The wide receiver was picked by the Bills in the first round of the 1979 NFL Draft, going fifth overall. The people in Clemson knew Jerry was special. He had made a spectacular catch in the closing minutes to give the Tigers a 1978 win over rival South Carolina and earn his team a trip to its first bowl game in 20 years.

It didn't take long for the Bills to recognize his speed and grace on the field, and he earned a starting job in no time in 1979. This game against the Jets was his coming-out party. He had a feeling something good might happen on this September day, even though he had a slightly separated shoulder.

"Joe [Ferguson] liked to pick on rookie defensive backs but I said, 'Hey, you have to know how to roll your dice because you've got a rookie receiver going against that rookie DB," Butler said to author Sal Maiorana. "But Joe just said, 'I can depend on you.'"

The game didn't start like the high-scoring free-for-all it would become. The first quarter featured few fireworks with three field goals, two by the Bills' Nick Mike-Mayer in taking a 6–3 lead. The Jets then responded in the second quarter with a pair of touchdown runs by Tom Newton. New York was up 17–6, and threatening to take control of the game.

That's where Butler started to go to work. Ferguson hit him with a 5-yard touchdown pass to cut the lead to five points. The Bills weren't even discouraged when the Jets answered with a scoring pass of their own to go up 24–12.

The Jets couldn't stop rookie receiver Jerry Butler in this matchup.
CREDIT ROBERT L. SMITH, ORCHARD PARK, NY

With only seven seconds left in the half, Ferguson threw a 75-yard pass to Butler for a touchdown off of a happy bounce. The ball was deflected by New York safety Burgess Owens but went right to Butler for the easy score. The Bills went into the half only trailing by 24–19.

"We worked on that 'Big Ben' play all the time in practice," guard Joe DeLamielleure said to Maiorana. "Somebody usually would say, 'What the hell are we practicing that play for?' And some other guy might say. 'Here we go again, now we're gonna waste five or 10 minutes on this damn thing.' But that practice sure paid off."

The third quarter was even better for the Bills. Butler caught another touchdown pass from Ferguson, this time for "only" 74 yards. The rookie fought off cornerback Johnny Lynn for the ball at the Bills' 45, and then ran untouched to the end zone for the score.

"It was supposed to be a screen, but I had the option of taking off depending on the coverage," Butler told Maiorana. "The ball was a little bit short. I remember slowing down a little bit and coming back inside, somewhat over the back of the shoulder. I think Lynn pretty much stumbled and wasn't able to recover to actually catch up with me. I swiped the ball and took it all the way in."

Two receptions for 149 yards and two touchdowns within minutes—that's a full day's work right there. Ferguson and Butler soon connected again, this time from 9 yards to make it 33–24. Defensive lineman Fred Smerlas got in the fun by returning a fumble 13 yards for a score. The Bills had scored 34 points in 30 minutes of play to go up 40–24. The game was essentially over.

Buffalo came away with a 46–31 win, as well as a rookie wide receiver who was the talk of the league that week. Butler finished with 10 catches for 255 yards and the four touchdowns; the yardage set a team record that lasted for about a quarter-century (Lee Evans eventually broke it). The 10 receptions were the most by a Bill since 1963, when Bill Miller had 12.

"That was the best single-game performance I've ever seen from a wide receiver," said television commentator and former NFL star John Brodie. "I played 16 years, but I've never seen anything like that. Ever."

Ranked No. 41 of 50 by the authors.

BOX SCORE

	1ST	2ND	3RD	4TH	FINAL
N.Y. JETS (L, 1-3)	3	21	0	7	31
BUFFALO (W, 2-2)	6	13	21	6	46

SCORING SUMMARY:

QTR	TEAM	PLAY
1ST	BUF.	Mike-Mayer 23-yard field goal
1ST	NYJ.	Leahy 30-yard field goal
1ST	BUF.	Mike-Mayer 29-yard field goal
2ND	NYJ.	Newton 51-yard run (Leahy kick)
2ND	NYJ.	Newton 1-yard run (Leahy kick)
2ND	BUF.	Ferguson 5-yard pass to Butler (kick blocked)
2ND	NYJ.	Todd 37-yard pass to Walker (Leahy kick)
2ND	BUF.	Ferguson 75-yard pass to Butler (Mike-Mayer kick)
3RD	BUF.	Ferguson 74-yard pass to Butler (Mike-Mayer kick)
3RD	BUF.	Ferguson 9-yard pass to Butler (Mike-Mayer kick)
3RD	BUF.	Smerlas 13-yard fumble return (Mike-Mayer kick)
4TH	BUF.	Ferguson 13-yard pass to Shipp (kick failed/bad snap)
4TH	NYJ.	Todd 27-yard pass to Shuler (Leahy kick)

ATTENDANCE: 68,731

NOTEWORTHY: *Ferguson had a memorable day himself, going 19 of 30 for 367 yards and five touchdowns. He was not intercepted. Newton had 68 yards rushing in eight carries, with 51 coming on one play. The teams combined for 913 yards in total offense. Buffalo's 497 yards set a stadium record. Those four scores were Butler's only touchdowns of the season, oddly enough. Smerlas's touchdown also was his only trip over the goal line in his long career.*

SEPTEMBER 7, 1980

DOLPHINS At BILLS

IN HINDSIGHT, it all seems ridiculous.

The Bills were placed in the same four-team division as the Miami Dolphins when the NFL fully integrated the teams from the American Football League for the 1970 season. That meant Buffalo would play Miami twice a year for the indefinite future.

They squared off 20 times during the course of the 1970s. Buffalo won exactly none of those games. In other words, the Bills went 0 for 20 to set a league record for consecutive losses to the same team. Forty-five years later it is still a league record in that category.

Happily for the Bills, a new decade and a fresh start came along in 1980. What's more, the team had shown improvement since Chuck Knox arrived as Buffalo's head coach for the 1978 season. The Bills went 5–11 in 1978 and 7–9 in 1979.

Yes, the Bills figured to be even better in 1980. But were they better than the Dolphins? That was the measuring stick that everyone used to grade the team. In other words, the attitude of many was "Call me when they beat the Dolphins." But just in case, Rich Stadium was sold out for the first time in five years for the season opener against Miami.

"There have been games where people expected a wide-open offensive game and it turned into a great defensive game, and vice versa," guard Reggie McKenzie of the Bills said before the game.

Head coach Chuck Knox received a ride off the field after his Bills finally knocked off the Dolphins.
CREDIT ROBERT L. SMITH, ORCHARD PARK, NY

"You never know with a battle between Miami and Buffalo, but you knew one thing—it's always a classic."

This contest was a classic for those who liked their football on the low-scoring side. The first half saw both teams struggle to move the football. Buffalo had the only score of the opening 30 minutes, a midrange field goal by Nick Mike-Mayer that was set up by an interception by Jeff Nixon. It was a sign that the Bills' defense was in top form on this day.

It took a bit of self-destruction for Miami

The goalposts did not survive the Bills' historic victory over the Dolphins.
CREDIT ROBERT L. SMITH, ORCHARD PARK, NY

to reach the scoreboard in the third quarter. A botched punt handed the Dolphins the ball on the Buffalo 27, and Bob Griese slipped a short pass to Tony Nathan for the go-ahead score. As the minutes counted down, it started to look like the lone Miami touchdown might be enough. The Bills even pulled off a fake punt for a big gain, only to see quarterback Joe Fergusion throw an interception—his fifth of the game.

There were no such mistakes on Buffalo's next possession, a 68-yard drive. The key play was a 29-yard pass from Ferguson to Jerry Butler with 3:56 left. Soon after that Ferguson flipped the ball to Roosevelt Leaks for a touchdown and the lead. No doubt someone in the stadium that day, having seen the previous 20 games, said, "Too much time."

Dolphins coach Don Shula replaced Griese with backup Don Strock, later citing Strock's stronger arm. That backfired, when Bills' linebacker Isiah Robertson intercepted the pass at midfield, and returned it all the way to the Miami 11. He said he thought he could score on the play "if it wasn't for the fact I stumbled on my last move."

From there, Cribbs took a handoff on a fourth-down play from the Dolphins' 1 and ran through a hole created by Conrad Dobler. Nixon made it virtually official a few plays later with his third interception of the game. Buffalo had a 17–7 victory.

It was not an offensive performance that belonged in the Albright-Knox Art Gallery. The numbers spoke volumes: nine penalties, five interceptions, two lost fumbles, and seven turnovers. Throw in some clock mismanagement, and the Bills appeared ready to make it 21 straight losses to Miami. Yet, they still won, and that made the result that much sweeter.

"It was a great win by a bunch of guys who were not going to be denied," Knox said. "I don't think I've ever seen a football team that came any more ready to play."

After the game, Bills' fans poured on to the field to celebrate. The goal posts soon felt victim to the assault. Those objects aren't cheap (about $2,000 each then), but Buffalo owner Ralph Wilson was in no mood to worry about that on this day. "It's the biggest win this club's ever had," he said. "Bigger than the AFL championships. I'll be happy to buy new goal posts."

"I had chills up and down my body as soon as I got to the top of the chute at the tunnel, that real good feeling you get from a big crowd like that," linebacker Phil Villapiano said. "It seemed like the old days in Oakland. The people really gave something to the guys and the guys gave something back to the people.

"Something like this can snowball. We can make something big out of this."

Ranked No. 3 of 50 by the authors.

BOX SCORE

	1ST	2ND	3RD	4TH	FINAL
MIAMI (L, 0-1)	0	0	7	0	7
BUFFALO (W, 1-0)	0	3	0	14	17

SCORING SUMMARY:

QTR	TEAM	PLAY
2ND	BUF.	Mike-Mayer 40-yard field goal
3RD	MIA.	Griese 4-yard pass to Nathan (von Schamann kick)
4TH	BUF.	Ferguson 4-yard pass to Leaks (Mike-Mayer kick)
4TH	BUF.	Cribbs 2-yard run (Mike Mayer kick)

ATTENDANCE: 79,598

NOTEWORTHY: *Both teams fumbled four times, and lost the ball twice on such plays. Cribbs had 60 yards rushing in his NFL debut, and caught nine passes for 71 yards. The number of receptions was a record for a Bills running back. Nixon's three interceptions tied a Bills record.*

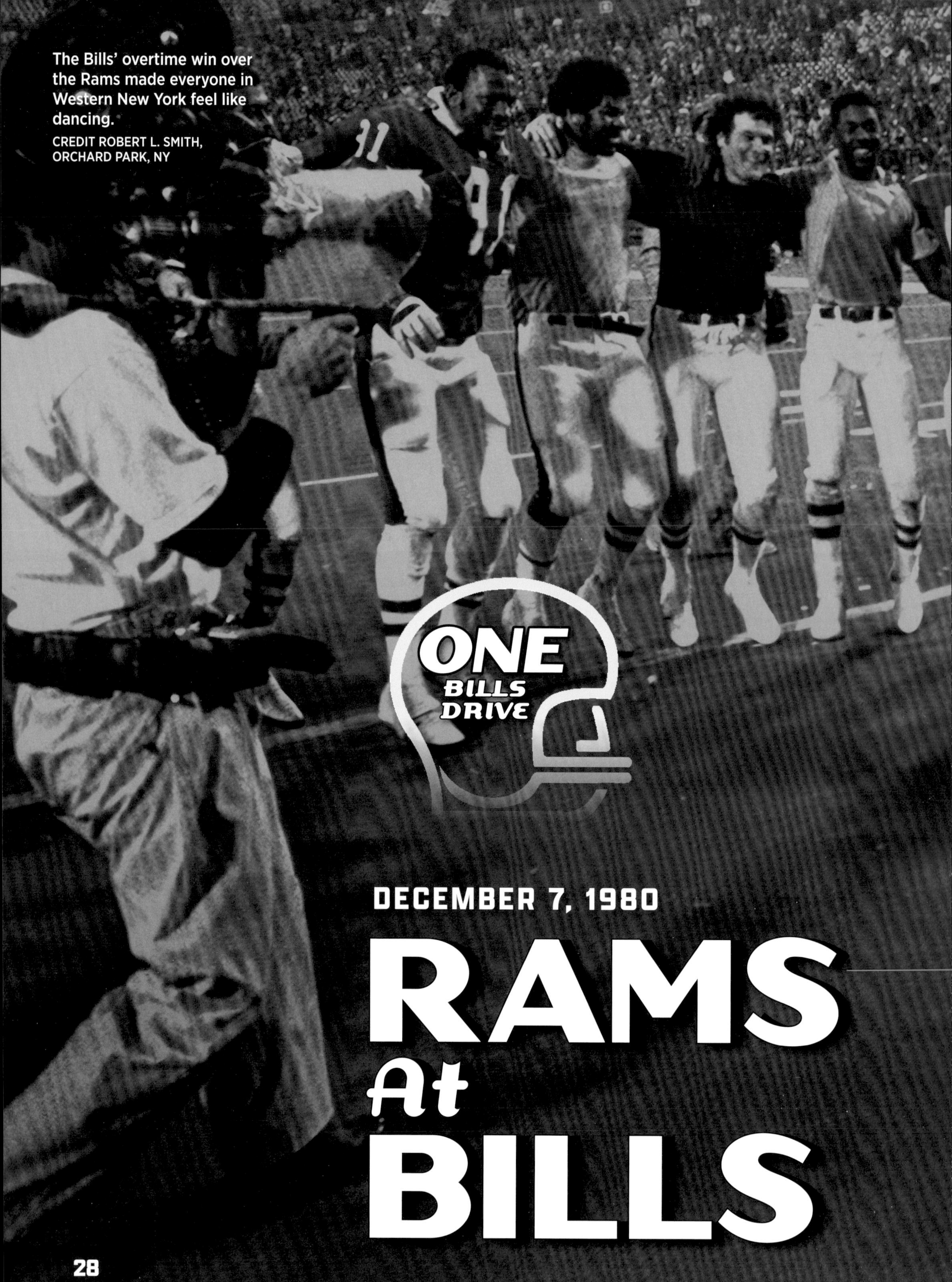

The Bills' overtime win over the Rams made everyone in Western New York feel like dancing.

CREDIT ROBERT L. SMITH, ORCHARD PARK, NY

DECEMBER 7, 1980

RAMS At BILLS

THE PHRASE "circle the calendar" is often used when a player in pro sports has his first chance to go up against his former team. The idea that it would be sweet to defeat that former organization and show that maybe, just maybe, keeping him would have been a good idea.

It's like that way for coaches, too.

Chuck Knox was the head coach of the Los Angeles Rams between 1973 and 1977. All he did there was win—at least 10 wins in all five seasons. But that wasn't really enough for Rams' owner Carroll Rosenbloom, who thought the team should have gone deeper into the playoffs (they never reached the Super Bowl) and should have played a more exciting style of football. Finally, Knox bolted for the Bills after the 1977 season.

The Bills had taken steps forward in Knox's first two years in Buffalo, and they were ready for another one in 1980. Buffalo won its first five games to show it was a legitimate contender to take the AFC East title that year. Later the Bills eventually played the game that Knox no doubt had circled on his calendar the moment the schedule came out: the Rams, in Buffalo, on December 7.

Knox was known for giving mostly vanilla quotes about games to the media, but there was little doubt that this one was particularly meaningful to him.

"I'm just preparing now as I would for another team," he said to NFL Films. "But I suppose on Sunday when we get on the field and I look out there and see those other guys I used to go to war with, and now I'm going to war against, it might be a different feeling."

The early December day in Rich Stadium wasn't particularly cold or windy, but the offenses certainly acted like it. Neither team could get on the scoreboard in the first half.

While Los Angeles did little, the Bills often self-destructed. In the second half, Buffalo finally put some points on the scoreboard. However, the offense had nothing to do with it. Rams quarterback Pat Haden's pass was intercepted by safety Steve Freeman, who ran 47 yards untouched for the touchdown.

The Rams answered with a score of their own later in the period. Mike Guman ran it in to climax an 80-yard drive, and Nolan Cromwell scrambled in with the extra point after a bad snap. That tied the game at 7–7, and that's when the frustration started to build on the Bills' sideline.

Buffalo's offense was stopped twice on fourth down inside the Rams' 10-yard line. Even worse, Joe Cribbs fumbled the ball away on the Rams' 11 with 1:08 remaining. It was time for the Bills' defense to go back to work.

"We shut them down, and the offense fumbled," linebacker Jim Haslett said. "Everyone on the sidelines looked at each other and grinned, and we went out and shut them down again."

At the start of overtime, Buffalo gained a couple of first downs and then it caught a break. Joe Ferguson's pass to Frank Lewis looked like it was going to be intercepted by LeRoy Irvin, but Lewis yanked it away from the defender and ran the ball to the Los Angeles 13. "It was the type of play (that) you might get it one out of 15 times," Lewis said.

Knox immediately sent in Nick Mike-Mayer to try a field goal. "We fumbled the ball down there before and I didn't want to take any chances," Knox said. "If we had a malfunction on the snap, we'd just eat the ball and try it again."

Mike-Mayer kicked the ball through the uprights—the biggest kick in his life, he said after the game—and Buffalo had a 10–7 win with 5:11 gone in overtime. The Bills celebrated for a while, and both teams headed for the locker rooms.

Then came the moment that everyone remembers. Most of the fans in the building stayed in their seats even though the game was over. Fans in the end zone started chanting "We want the Bills!"

After a few minutes, about half of the team responded by stopping what they were doing, and going back on to the field in various stages of undress. Some of them joined the team's cheerleaders, the Buffalo Jills, for an impromptu line dance of sorts. It was spontaneous, and it was magical.

"People weren't leaving, so I thought I'd come out and say hello and really thank them for their support throughout the game," Mike-Mayer said on the field during the celebration. "I hope they stay out there all night and party."

Knox gave a clue about his feelings for the game. He decided to give everyone on the roster a game ball, an unusual gesture. But his players responded with an even more unusual gesture. They said there would be only one game ball on this day, and Knox would receive it.

"The man wanted this one in the worst way," guard Reggie McKenzie said.

Ranked No. 16 of 50 by the authors.

BOX SCORE

	1ST	2ND	3RD	4TH	OT	FINAL
L.A. RAMS (L, 9-5)	0	0	7	0	0	7
BUFFALO (W, 10-4)	0	0	7	0	3	10

SCORING SUMMARY:

QTR	TEAM	PLAY
3RD	BUF.	Freeman 47-yard interception return (Mike-Mayer kick)
3RD	LAR.	Guman 3-yard run (Cromwell run)
OT	BUF.	Mike-Mayer 30-yard field goal

ATTENDANCE: 77,133

NOTEWORTHY: *The Rams' quarterbacks had a miserable day. Vince Ferragamo was 3 of 7 for 20 yards before leaving the game with injured ribs. Haden came on in relief, and was 5 of 16 for 41 yards and an interception. Buffalo's Ferguson wasn't much better—10 of 25 for 138 yards. Neither side had a 100-yard rusher. The win was also enjoyed by an ex-Ram linebacker on the Bills' roster, Isiah Robertson. "I had a bad time in L.A. from being a victim of circumstances," he said. "But it all washes out in the end. We're on top and now they're on the bottom, but I'm sorry I had to be the one to knock them out."*

NOVEMBER 22, 1981

PATRIOTS At BILLS

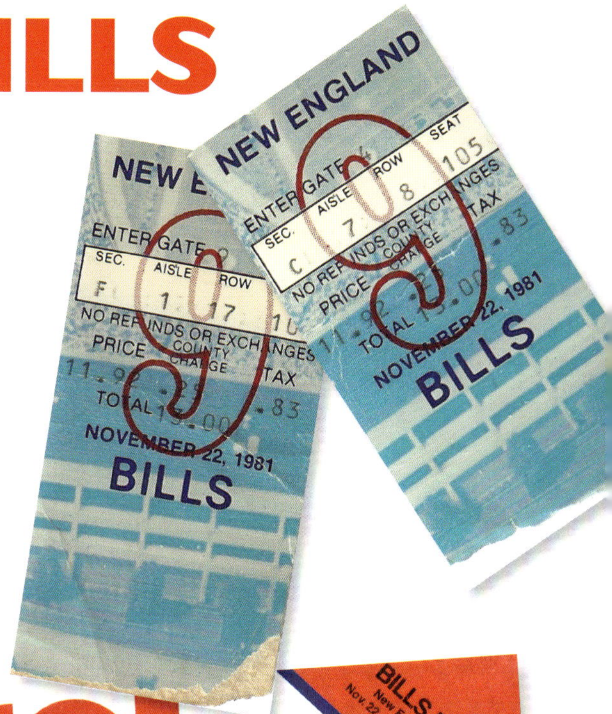

AFTER A storybook 1980 season that saw the Bills win the division and reach the NFL playoffs, the 1981 season had been a struggle up until this point. Buffalo had opened with a couple of one-sided wins, but then settled into mediocrity. The Bills had lost games in Dallas and St. Louis earlier in November, with the Cardinals winning in a discouraging 24–0 rout. If the Bills were going to return to the postseason, they needed to achieve some consistency.

Holding on to the football would be one way to achieve that goal. There were 11 Buffalo turnovers in the two losses to the opponents from the NFC, and that was unacceptable.

"We've got to quit turning the ball over and we have to tackle and hit better on defense," Bills' head coach Chuck Knox said.

The Patriots figured to be a good place to start. For a team that missed on a playoff spot by a single game in 1980, New England was a major disappointment a season later. It had lost four straight games to fall to 2–9 on the season, and their games had become tryouts for next year. The Pats had a couple of dangerous offensive players in Stanley Morgan and Tony Collins, but little else. The team had allowed 35 sacks already in the 1981 season.

"I don't consider us playing the spoiler," Patriots' safety Tim Fox said. "I feel it is our job to go out and try to win football games, and that's what we will do against the Bills. As far as I'm concerned, we're playing for pride."

New England's problems moving the ball popped up in the first 30 minutes, and it had

BOX SCORE

	1ST	2ND	3RD	4TH	FINAL
NEW ENGLAND (L, 2-10)	7	0	3	7	17
BUFFALO (W, 7-5)	3	10	0	7	20

SCORING SUMMARY:

QTR	TEAM	PLAY
1ST	BUF.	Mike-Mayer 28-yard field goal
1ST	N.E.	Johnson 56-yard pass to Morgan (Smith kick)
2ND	BUF.	Mike-Mayer 23-yard field goal
2ND	BUF.	Ferguson 11-yard pass to Hooks (Mike-Mayer kick)
3RD	N.E.	Smith 43-yard field goal
4TH	N.E.	Cavanaugh 5-yard pass to Hasselbeck (Smith kick)
4TH	BUF.	Ferguson 36-yard pass to Hooks (Mike-Mayer kick)

ATTENDANCE: 71,593

one offensive moment in the first half—and it was a trick play. Andy Johnson threw a 56-yard option pass to Morgan for a touchdown. That gave the Pats a 7–3 lead in the first quarter. After Nick Mike-Mayer kicked his second field goal of the day and Joe Ferguson threw a touchdown pass to Roland Hooks, the Bills seemed in control.

But the Patriots weren't done yet. John Smith's field goal moved New England within three points at 13–10, and Matt Cavanaugh hit Don Hasselbeck for 5 yards and a touchdown. Now the Bills trailed by 17–13, and only 1:56 remained. Things looked worse for Buffalo when the Patriots' Rick Sanford intercepted a pass with 1:32 to go. But a defensive stop and a punt gave the Bills one last chance with 35 seconds left.

Ferguson threw to Hooks, who made a leaping, lunging grab for a 37-yard gain to put the ball in New England territory. The quarterback had to throw the ball out of bounds to stop the clock, so that left only 12 seconds left. Ferguson threw what has become known as a "Hail Mary" pass into a strong wind and into the end zone . . . because they are so unlikely to be completed that sometimes help from other sources is needed. Buffalo's formal name for it was "90 All

Sometimes prayers are answered—in this case, by Bills' receiver Roland Hooks.
CREDIT ROBERT L. SMITH, ORCHARD PARK, NY

Go." A completion seemed unlikely but at least possible to Hooks.

"I don't ever remember playing a game, particularly a close game, where we have a chance of winning, thinking, 'We can't do this,'" he said to author Jim Gehman later. "Particularly on offense, we were pretty confident that we could get the job done."

This time, Hooks answered the prayer. Either Mike Hawkins, a New England linebacker, or Bills receiver Frank Lewis (accounts differ) tipped the ball, and it landed in Hooks' arms for the game-winning touchdown. It was one of the greatest—and most unexpected—finishes in the history of the Bills.

"I was happy it was me," Hooks said. "I saw the ball the whole way. It was a desperation pass. I was left alone to the side and nobody bumped me."

"It's one of those plays we work on," Knox said. "But you just don't hit them like that."

The team's defensive players felt the same joy and relief as their offensive counterparts.

"I was praying and thinking, what am I going to say to the press?" cornerback Mario Clark said.

"The executioner had the switch halfway down, it was 12 o'clock and then the governor came down with a reprieve," safety Bill Simpson added.

Just like that, the Bills were 7–5 on the season, and their playoff hopes were taken off life support. "It picks us up, it's a morale booster," Ferguson said. "We honestly can't lose another game if we want to get into the playoffs."

Ranked No. 10 of 50 by the authors.

NOTEWORTHY: *Hooks led the Bills with six catches for 111 yards to go with the two touchdowns. He also chipped in with 45 yards rushing. The veteran came on in relief of Joe Cribbs, who injured his ribs early in the game. Ferguson was 15 of 34 for 258 yards. Matt Cavanaugh only threw 12 passes, completing six of them for 133 yards. Sixty-five of those yards came on a bomb to Stanley Morgan shortly before the touchdown pass to Don Hasselbeck.*

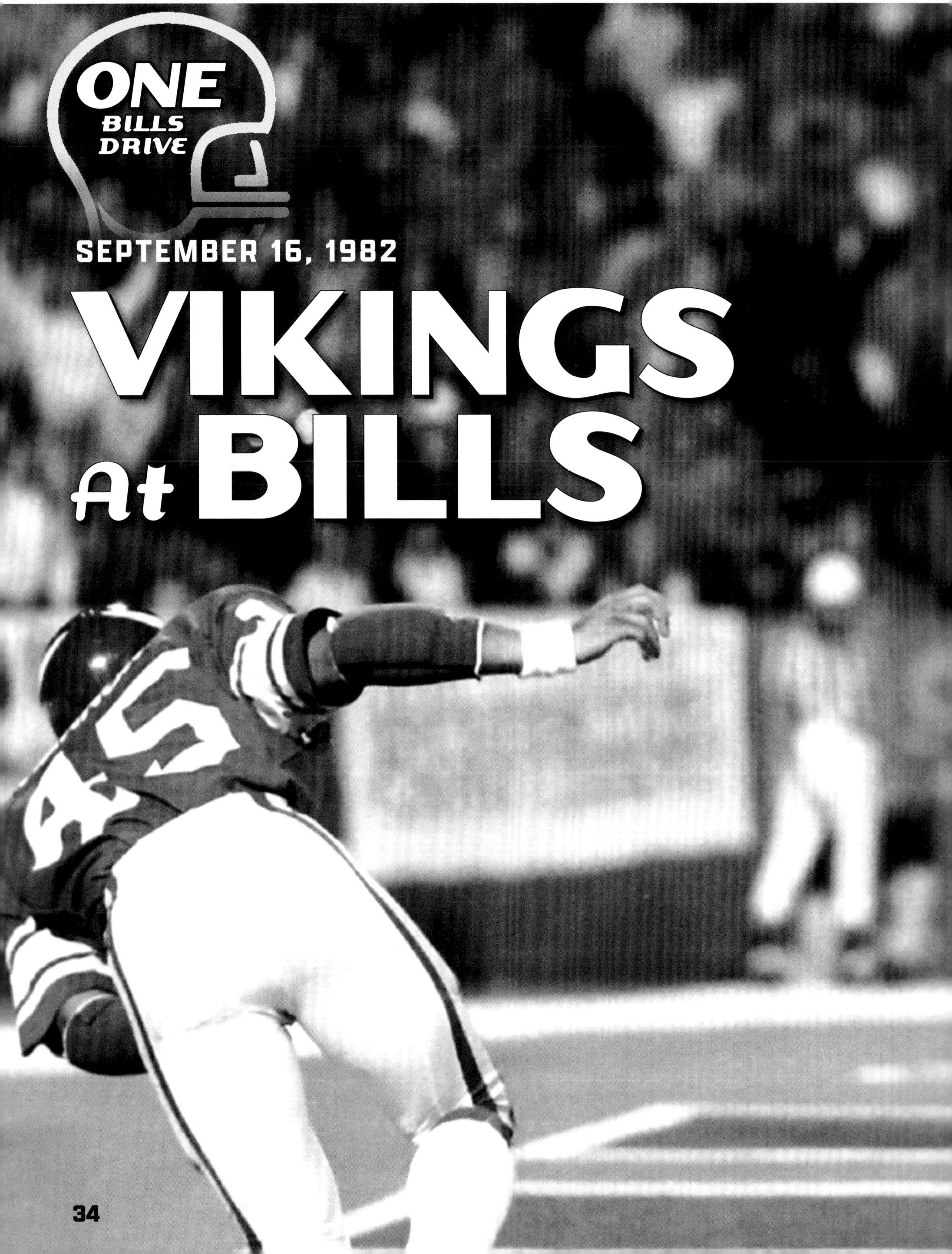
ONE BILLS DRIVE
SEPTEMBER 16, 1982
VIKINGS At BILLS

A SENSE of foreboding surrounded this Thursday night game between the Bills and the Vikings, which would start the second week of the NFL season. The players and owners had been unable to reach a collective bargaining agreement since the old deal expired on July 15, and there was talk of a strike. The Players Association had figured out that a walkout during the middle of the season would be more damaging to the owners than one in training camp, so they were prepared to strike as soon as week two was over—in other words, on the Tuesday after the week's contests.

"The date has been set," a source told the Associated Press. "It shouldn't come as that much of a surprise to anyone."

A strike in midseason would be historic and significant. The only walkout in NFL history had come in 1974, when the players stayed out of training camp. Now in 1982, games would have to be postponed or cancelled.

As could be expected, the talk of a strike dampened enthusiasm for the prime-time telecast of the game between two teams with playoff hopes. With positions hardened, no one knew when the next Bills' game would be. Then the game started, and it was easy to wonder if Buffalo had started a walkout a few days early.

The first half completely belonged to Minnesota. The Vikings started the game with a safety, and then added a pair of touchdowns on throws from Tommy Kramer to Bob Bruer. The Bills looked tired, confused, and perhaps a bit distracted.

Buffalo's comedy of errors continued with Arthur Whittington's fumble that the Vikings recovered on the Minnesota 34-yard line. It resulted in a field goal, and the Vikings were in complete control with a 19–0 lead. "We were befuddled more than we were tired," Bills nose tackle Fred Smerlas said. "They threw so much stuff at us we had a hard time figuring out what to do."

The Bills finally broke through late in the first half with a drive that ended with a short touchdown pass from Joe Ferguson to Frank Lewis with 14 seconds left. Buffalo kept the momentum in the second half, with Ferguson finding Jerry Butler for a score. Minnesota responded with a field goal to go up 22–13.

On the first play of the final quarter, Nick Mike-Mayer booted a 21-yard field goal to cap a 76-yard drive in 14 plays. The Bills

Jerry Butler's second touchdown catch of the day capped a furious Buffalo rally.
CREDIT ROBERT L. SMITH, ORCHARD PARK, NY

converted a fourth-and-one from their own 30-yard line to keep the scoring drive alive. "No, there was no hesitation on the fourth and one," Bills head coach Chuck Knox said. "Our reason was we had been moving the ball so well that we felt we needed a couple of big plays. It was one of them. It's not a percentage play. We had to make it and we felt that way and we went ahead and made it."

Down by six points, the Bills opened a drive with 7:37 left 94 yards away from the goal line. Ferguson completed a huge 39-yard pass to Lewis to the Minnesota 15. "Frank Lewis made a big catch," Knox said. "There was an excellent throw and you have to make big plays like that against an opponent as good as Minnesota."

Ferguson soon followed that play with a touchdown pass to Butler that tied the game. Mike-Mayer booted the all-important extra point, and the Bills had come all the way back from a 19-point deficit to take the lead, 23–22. "There was really nothing to think about," Mike-Mayer said. "You just kick it."

Minnesota had two more chances to regain the lead, but the Bills' defense stiffened to secure the victory.

"Maybe Chuck Knox is changing," Ferguson said of the Bills' usually conservative coach. "It was a game in which there were a lot of opportunities for coaches to make decisions. He took the risk, made the gamble. I am proud of him."

Once the game ended, everyone's attention immediately turned to the possibility of a strike. "Our team is together. We will move as a team," Bills player representative Lou Piccone said.

Ferguson wasn't too optimistic. "I hope this [comment] goes around the world," he said to reporters. "I hope the owners get off their high horses, and I hope the union will get off its high horse and settle this thing. There has to be a happy medium somewhere."

There wasn't. The players went on strike on September 21, and stayed out for 57 days—the longest labor dispute in NFL history.

Ranked No. 48 of 50 by the authors.

BOX SCORE

	1ST	2ND	3RD	4TH	FINAL
MINNESOTA (L, 1-1)	2	17	3	0	22
BUFFALO (W, 2-0)	0	7	6	10	23

SCORING SUMMARY:

QTR	TEAM	PLAY
1ST	MIN.	Safety, Mullaney tackled Moore in end zone
2ND	MIN.	Kramer 22-yard pass to Bruer (Danmeier kick)
2ND	MIN.	Kramer 2-yard pass to Bruer (Danmeier kick)
2ND	MIN.	Danmeier 43-yard field goal
2ND	BUF.	Ferguson 6-yard pass to Lewis (Mike-Mayer kick)
3RD	BUF.	Ferguson 4-yard pass to Butler (kick failed)
3RD	MIN.	Danmeier 42-yard field goal
4TH	BUF.	Mike-Mayer 21-yard field goal
4TH	BUF.	Ferguson 11-yard pass to Butler (Mike-Mayer kick)

ATTENDANCE: 77,753

NOTEWORTHY: *Bills' star running back Joe Cribbs sat out the game in a contract dispute. Roosevelt Leaks was the team's leading rusher in Cribbs' absence with 76 yards on 13 carries. Ferguson had one of his best days as a pro, completing 25 of 45 passes for 330 yards and three touchdowns. It was the Bills' first ever regular season win over Minnesota, after three losses. The Vikings set a team record with 15 penalties for 117 yards.*

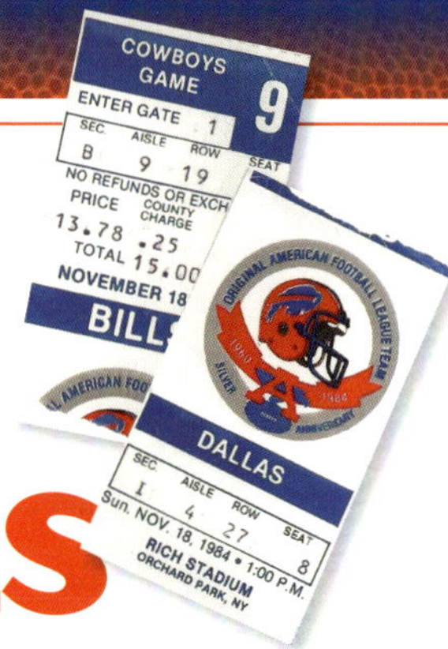

NOVEMBER 18, 1984

COWBOYS At BILLS

IF THE START of the 1984 season wasn't the lowest point in the history of the Buffalo Bills, it's tough to guess what was.

The Bills had been a playoff contender under Chuck Knox in the early 1980s, but they fell on hard times after he left for Seattle. Kay Stephenson took over a team that was crumbling, falling to 8-8 in 1983. But no one expected the Bills to start the season with 11—that's right, 11—straight losses. Three of those games were 30-point losses, and another came by 28 points. They had given up 322 points, tops in the league.

The fans had waived the white flag too. Fewer than 40,000 turned out for home games on October 7, October 21, and November 4. Some of the Bills' backers, though, were simply saving their money, because "America's Team" was coming to town later in the season. That was the nickname of the Dallas Cowboys in that era, given to the team by NFL Films.

The Cowboys weren't always great, but they were usually at least good. As a result, they became one of the most popular teams in the league nationwide. In this particular year, the Cowboys were struggling a bit. They came into the game with a 7–4 record, not up to their usual standards. Dallas had lost three of its previous six games. Still, the team was enough of an attraction to almost fill Rich Stadium. The Cowboys brought such players as Tony Dorsett, Ed "Too Tall" Jones, Randy White, and Everson Walls to town for their first-ever game in Rich Stadium.

Those expecting a one-sided result didn't need to wait long to be surprised. The Bills had the ball on the 15-yard line after the opening kickoff. Greg Bell took a handoff from Joe Ferguson, found a hole, and took off. Suddenly, Bell had nothing but open space in front of him. The rookie raced 85 yards for a touchdown, and the Bills found themselves in front.

Greg Bell heads for the goal line on an 85-yard run against the Cowboys.
CREDIT ROBERT L. SMITH, ORCHARD PARK, NY

Joe Ferguson didn't have a great game throwing the ball, but Greg Bell's running more than compensated for it.
CREDIT GETTY IMAGES

"The funny thing is, before the game I told Booker Moore that I had a dream that I broke a long run, the length of the field for a touchdown on the first play of the game," Bell said later. "Booker looked at me and said, 'I had the same dream. Now let's go make it happen.'"

Those wearing Cowboys apparel in the stands probably thought Bell's run would serve as a big wake-up call for a team that needed one. But it seemed that few people heard it. Dallas struggled on offense throughout the day. Gary Hogeboom, remembered as one of those unfortunate quarterbacks who had Roger Staubach on one side of him on the team's historical timeline and Troy Aikman on the other, had some good moments. He completed 22 of 45 passes for 242 yards, but was intercepted twice and was sacked three times. Hogeboom was playing in place of Danny White, who had been benched.

BOX SCORE

	1ST	2ND	3RD	4TH	FINAL
DALLAS (L, 7-5)	0	3	0	0	3
BUFFALO (W, 1-11)	7	0	0	7	14

SCORING SUMMARY:

QTR	TEAM	PLAY
1ST	BUF.	Bell 85-yard run (Nelson kick)
2ND	DAL.	Septien 20-yard field goal
4TH	BUF.	Ferguson 3-yard pass to Bell (Nelson kick)

ATTENDANCE: 79,598

As for the Dallas running game, it was held to a standstill by a surprising Bills defense. Dorsett finished with 70 yards, and the team finished with 78 for the day—seven yards behind Bell's gain from the opening run.

The Cowboys did kick a field goal in the second quarter to narrow Buffalo's lead to four. Everyone in the building, no doubt, expected Dallas to figure out a way to beat the Bills . . . because, in that season, the Bills always lost. Yet it was the Dallas defense that finally cracked. Bell scored again in the fourth quarter, this time on a short pass from Ferguson, and the lead was a much safer 14–3. It held up for the rest of the game.

Bell finished the day with 27 carries for 206 yards. The rest of the team was a combined minus-three in rushing yards. Reactions were exactly what you'd think they would be:

"I feel like we're leading the league," Bills owner Ralph Wilson said.

"It was not a good show," said Dallas coach Tom Landry. "We deserved what we got. It was somewhat embarrassing. It's always embarrassing when you lose. It was not one of our better hours."

It could be argued that this was the most unexpected result in Bills history covering games played at One Bills Drive. The only bigger surprise in team history might have come in 1968, when Buffalo shocked the New York Jets, 37–35, in War Memorial Stadium. The Jets won the Super Bowl that year, while the Bills won no other games in 1968.

Ranked No. 17 of 50 by the authors.

NOTEWORTHY: *Bell's first score was the longest run from scrimmage ever given up by the Cowboys at the time, and it was the third-longest run from scrimmage in Bills history at that moment. Bell also became the first runner to gain 200 yards against the Cowboys since Jim Brown did it in 1963. Bell ran for exactly 1,100 yards that season. Ferguson was 13 of 29 for 117 yards with two interceptions and two sacks. At halftime, former Buffalo quarterback Jack Kemp became the second Bills player placed on the team's Wall of Fame. Before the game, some of the Bills' players had collected money for a large postgame party in case the team upset the Cowboys. According to Fred Smerlas' autobiography,* By a Nose, *the party turned out to be "legendary."*

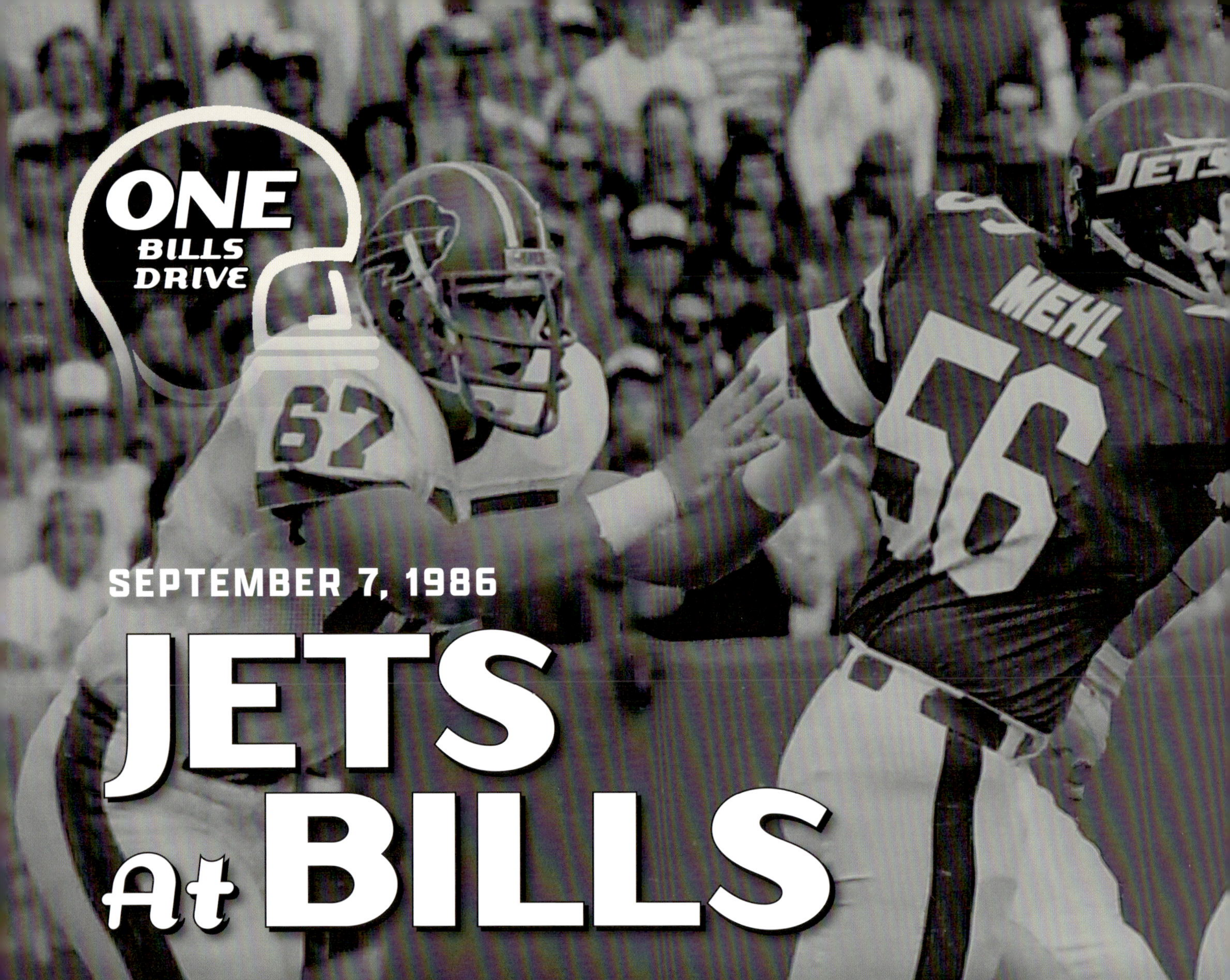

ONE BILLS DRIVE

SEPTEMBER 7, 1986

JETS At BILLS

THE BUFFALO BILLS weren't selling tickets to their first home game of the 1986 NFL season. They were selling hope.

The Bills hadn't been above .500 since 1981 at this point. They were coming off a pair of 2–14 seasons that featured a parade of forgettable faces, particularly at quarterback.

But a few weeks before the opener, the Bills signed a passer named Jim Kelly to a contract that made him the highest-paid player in the NFL. Kelly had been with the United States Football League, which had folded. The Bills finally had signed their first-round draft choice from 1983. The fans voted to approve the move with their wallets. They bought 10,000 season tickets in the week after the signing.

Now, after some preseason work, it was time to see what this heralded quarterback could do. The Jets were a good team at that point, coming off an 11–5 season. The result didn't really matter in this situation. An almost completely filled Rich Stadium couldn't wait to see what the Bills had in Kelly, although one fan had an idea. It was tough to miss the banner that read "Kelly Is God." Jeffrey Green of suburban Rochester was identified decades later as the person who constructed the sign. He admitted that the message was rather over the top, and that he was a bit carried away with the excitement of the debut

Jim Kelly's arrival in Orchard Park was a sign of good things to come.
CREDIT ROBERT L. SMITH, ORCHARD PARK, NY

of Kelly, who didn't appreciate the sentiment.

When Kelly was introduced before the game, the fans let out a yell that still might be bouncing around the grounds of the stadium. "I had chills all over my body," Kelly said. "I was excited. But to tell the truth, when I was in the USFL, I was more nervous in a few games than I was out there today."

The rest of the day wasn't much quieter, including the times that Kelly was on the sidelines. "I had to look at the ball a lot of times to see when it was snapped," Jets' offensive tackle Jim Sweeney said.

It didn't take long for Kelly to have an impact. His first pass was a completion to tight end Pete Metzelaars. Kelly's first touchdown pass in the NFL came in the first quarter—a 1-yard toss to running back Greg Bell. The Jets eventually answered with a pair of touchdowns, including a long pass from quarterback Ken O'Brien to receiver Al Toon. The Bills came close to tying the game shortly after that, but the drive stalled with eight seconds left in the half. Coach Hank Bullough opted to kick a field goal; Scott Norwood made it a 14–10 Jets' lead.

Along the way, Kelly received a rough introduction into the NFL. He was knocked into something close to dreamland in the first half. "I didn't even know where I was," Kelly said after the game. But he returned for the second half.

There was no scoring in the third quarter, but the first tally of the final period gave us a glimpse into the future. Kelly hit Andre Reed with a 55-yard touchdown pass, and the Bills had a 17–14 lead. That combination would become one of the most fruitful in NFL history, and eventually would go all the way to Canton, Ohio, and the Pro Football Hall of Fame.

The Jets, though, weren't impressed, scoring two more touchdowns. The second came on a bomb from O'Brien to Wesley Walker, who beat Bills' cornerback Derrick Burroughs. "I thought the ball hit me in the back of the head, or that I might've knocked it down," the defender said. "Then I looked up and he was heading down the sideline."

That insurance policy came in handy when Kelly threw another TD pass. The Jets still led by four points with 3:55 left, so the Bills needed a defensive stop in order to have one last chance at winning.

"The offense wanted the ball back so bad," Kelly said. "We were pumped up. We wanted the chance to run our two-minute offense and score. We wanted to win this game. We just did not get the ball back."

The Jets simply ran out the clock. The big play came when O'Brien found Toon for a 12-yard gain with 1:32 left in a third-and-11 situation. That was the game; New York was a 28–24 winner.

At least the days of players such as Bruce Matheson and Joe Dufek starting at quarterback were over for another decade. A new sheriff was in town. That first look at Kelly is why this game is so memorable for all concerned. He finished 20 of 33 for 292 yards and three touchdowns with no interceptions.

Good times were coming.

Ranked No. 27 of 50 by the authors.

BOX SCORE

	1ST	2ND	3RD	4TH	FINAL
N.Y. JETS (W, 1-0)	7	7	0	14	28
BUFFALO (L, 0-1)	7	3	0	14	24

SCORING SUMMARY:

QTR	TEAM	PLAY
1ST	BUF.	Kelly 1-yard pass to Bell (Norwood kick)
1ST	NYJ.	Paige 2-yard run (Leahy kick)
2ND	NYJ.	O'Brien 46-yard pass to Toon (Leahy kick)
2ND	BUF.	Norwood 19-yard field goal
4TH	BUF.	Kelly 55-yard pass to Reed (Norwood kick)
4TH	NYJ.	Hector 1-yard run (Leahy kick)
4TH	NYJ.	O'Brien 71-yard pass to Walker (Leahy kick)
4TH	BUF.	Kelly 4-yard pass to Metzelaars (Norwood kick)

ATTENDANCE: 79,951

NOTEWORTHY: *Bell led the Bills in rushing with 44 yards on 17 carries. Reed had five catches for 95 yards, while Metzelaars had four receptions. No Bills quarterback had thrown three touchdowns in a game since Joe Ferguson did it against the Jets in 1983. Safety Steve Freeman became the second Bills player in history to that point to participate in 12 different seasons. The other was Joe Ferguson. The attendance of 79,951 set a regular-season team record. Buffalo drew 80,020 for the stadium's opening game—a preseason contest with Washington.*

OCTOBER 18, 1987

GIANTS At BILLS

ONE OF THE WORST games in modern NFL history was played between the New York Giants and the Buffalo Bills. That's a big statement, but the game lived up to it.

Rich Stadium was less than a fifth full when the "counterfeit" Bills (and Giants) battled for more than four quarters. The teams were playing the last of three replacement games caused by the NFL players' strike. The 24-day labor action had ended prior to that weekend's games but the owners agreed that a final weekend of replacement games would be played. Most of the regular players would return for games on October 25.

Of the 44 Bills players who played in this game, only four from their regular roster crossed the picket line. For the Giants, three of 41 were from the original roster. However, one was superstar linebacker Lawrence Taylor and another was veteran NFL quarterback Jeff Rutledge. Of the 85 players that played in the game, 72 of them had only played replacement football as professionals.

Coming into this game both the Bills and Giants had lost their first two replacement games. The Bills had been outscored 61 to 13. The Giants had been outscored 79 to 33 and had allowed the most points of all the replacement teams. The front offices of the two franchises opted not to put much effort into forming a substitute team in the hope that relations with the striking regulars could be salvaged once the settlement was reached. But these games did count in the

Quarterback Brian McClure's solitary pro game proved to be a memorable one.
CREDIT ROBERT L. SMITH, ORCHARD PARK, NY

standings, adding a layer of importance to the last NFL contest featuring the substitute rosters.

The first quarter saw the Giants fumble the ball three times, though they recovered each one, as they were unable to generate any offense. The Bills were able to move the ball into Giants' territory midway through the first quarter, but halfback Robb Riddick fumbled at the New York 13-yard line and the Giants recovered.

Bills quarterback Brian McClure, a former team draft choice who was signed solely to play in this game, threw interceptions on the Bills' next two possessions, and Rutledge threw one for the Giants.

The final six minutes of the second quarter was filled with penalties, incomplete passes, sacks, unsuccessful running plays, and punts. The half ended with McClure's third interception of the game and the teams left the field with the score tied at zero. At one point, the game was such a mess that Giants' general manager George Young, who was sitting in the press box, needed to wipe tears off his glasses from his laughter over the hijinks in front of him.

In the third quarter, Todd Schlopy missed a field goal, and the Bills fumbled on another possession for their fifth turnover. The quarter ended with the score knotted 0–0, and the first scoreless tie in the NFL since World War II seemed quite possible.

The Giants drove the ball into Bills' territory early in the fourth quarter, but kicker George Benyola missed a 37-yard field goal. On the next play, the Bills fumbled the ball back to New York. The Bills defense held, and this time Benyola made a 22-yard field goal to give the Giants what seemed like an almost insurmountable 3–0 lead with 9:38 remaining.

BOX SCORE

	1ST	2ND	3RD	4TH	OT	FINAL
N.Y. GIANTS (L, 0-5)	0	0	0	3	0	3
BUFFALO (W, 2-3)	0	0	0	3	3	6

SCORING SUMMARY:

QTR	TEAM	PLAY
4TH	NYG.	Benyola 22-yard field goal
4TH	BUF.	Schlopy 31-yard field goal
OT	BUF.	Schlopy 27-yard field goal

ATTENDANCE: 15,737

The Bills responded with an all-important 56-yard drive, and Schlopy finished it with a 31-yard field goal to tie the game. New York missed a game-winning field goal with little time left that had been set up by a Bills fumble, and the contest went to overtime.

In the extra session, the Bills had three chances to make a field goal to win the game. The first two failed, one on a fumbled snap and the other because the kick was wide left. But with only 22 seconds remaining in the overtime period, Schlopy got one last chance. This time, his 27-yard field goal attempt was true, and it delivered the Bills a 6–3 victory.

The last word belonged to running back Carl Byrum, who had crossed the picket line to play. When asked what he was thinking when Schlopy lined up for the final kick, Byrum replied, "Help me out here. Who's Schlopy?"

Ranked No. 32 of 50 by the authors.

NOTEWORTHY: *The game lasted 3 hours and 52 minutes. The winning Bills had three passes intercepted, five fumbles with four lost, eleven penalties for 113 yards with seven of those holding penalties on Taylor and three missed field goals and one aborted on a bad snap. The losing Giants had two passes intercepted, four fumbles, two missed field goals, 15 penalties for 145 yards, and punted ten times. Byrum finished with 139 yards on 25 carries. It was the only time in his three-year NFL career that he ran for 50 yards, let alone 100. McClure holds three obscure NFL records from this game. He has the most yards passing, 181, the most completions, 20, and the most attempts, 38, for any quarterback in NFL history that only played a single game.*

NOVEMBER 20, 1988

JETS At BILLS

THE BUFFALO BILLS had plenty of highs and lows during the 1980s, and Fred Smerlas was part of almost all of them.

Smerlas arrived as a second-round draft choice in 1979. He was part of a rebuilding program under head coach Chuck Knox, who had arrived in the previous year to try to fix what had become an absolute mess of the team. Smerlas was part of a draft class that also featured Jerry Butler, Jim Haslett and Jon Borchardt. It was a good group, even if the team's front office couldn't sign the No. 1 overall draft pick, Tom Cousineau.

Smerlas was a key part of the Bills' team that won the AFC East in 1980 and made it to the playoffs in 1981. But the former Boston College standout found out that good times don't last in the NFL, as the Bills crash-landed in the middle of the 1980s. Hope returned in 1986 with the arrival of quarterback Jim Kelly and head coach Marv Levy. By 1988, the Bills were ready to be a contender.

Buffalo opened the season with four straight wins, lost a game in Chicago, and then won six more contests. That put the Bills at 10–1 entering a November date with the New York Jets at Rich Stadium. Almost amazingly, Buffalo would clinch the division title with a win over the Jets—which Levy didn't want to be a distraction. "We're focusing on the New York Jets," he said. No NFL team had ever clinched a division title so early in the football calendar.

What no one knew about that game ahead of time is that it would provide Smerlas with the most memorable moment of his career.

It was a difficult day to be a player or a fan in Orchard Park. Temperatures were in the low 40s, and rain and sleet provided the backdrop. Both offenses were generally ineffective,

The fans stormed the field after the Bills wrapped up the AFC East title.
CREDIT ROBERT L. SMITH, ORCHARD PARK, NY

especially in getting the ball over the goal line. The matchup became something of a pitchers' duel, with both sides realizing that any score would have a large impact on the game.

The Jets scored first, as Pat Leahy kicked a short field goal in the second quarter. It was the only points of the opening 30 minutes. The Bills' Scott Norwood matched that play in the third period, so the teams went into the fourth quarter tied 3–3.

The tension ramped up. Norwood put the Bills ahead with another kick from close range, but Leahy did the same. Then the Jets moved the ball into position for what figured to be the game-winning field goal. Leahy only had to convert from 40 yards, and the Jets would delay the division-clinching party by at least a week. Leahy was a dependable kicker, having made 38 of his previous 40 kicks from inside 40 yards.

With 25 seconds left, the Jets snapped the ball, Leahy kicked it . . . and Smerlas stormed up the middle to block the kick.

"I had a strange feeling we were going to block it. I really did," Smerlas said. "The field goal before, they had given me a gap. They were blocking down to block off inside pressure and I hit a gapper. I figured if I turned sidewards, I'd be able to penetrate far enough maybe to get a piece of it. Fortunately, I did. I think it hit my hand and hit 'The House" [Howard Ballard] on the head."

The game soon moved into overtime, and cornerback Derrick Burroughs made a big play of his own. He caused a fumble by the Jets' Roger Vick on their second play of extra time. Cornelius Bennett recovered the ball. The Bills quickly moved into field-goal range. Norwood came through again from 30 yards away, and Buffalo claimed its first AFC East title in eight years.

The celebration began immediately, and not just from the players. The fans, many clad in yellow and orange rain gear, came on to the field to join in the celebration. The goalposts soon came down.

"I just saw about 10 of them, and I didn't think anything of it at first," Bills' tight end Pete Metzelaars said about the fans. "The next thing I knew, there was a hundred out there. And then a thousand. And then I started worrying if I was ever going to get off the field. When I finally did get off the field and into the tunnel, I just stopped, turned around and watched. . . . It was an amazing thing to see."

But the win might never have happened without the play of Smerlas—a great reward for a decade of good work as a Bill. He had his own unique way of describing the game: "There's nothing sweeter than to win in front of the home crowd. We deserved it and Buffalo deserved it. We had that welcome sign on our back for so many years, it's about time we get it washed off."

Ranked No. 12 of 50 by the authors.

BOX SCORE

	1ST	2ND	3RD	4TH	OT	FINAL
N.Y. JETS (L, 5-6-1)	0	3	0	3	0	6
BUFFALO (W, 11-1)	0	0	3	3	3	9

SCORING SUMMARY:

QTR	TEAM	PLAY
2ND	NYJ.	Leahy 23-yard field goal
3RD	BUF.	Norwood 25-yard field goal
4TH	BUF.	Norwood 26-yard field goal
4TH	NYJ.	Leahy 40-yard field goal
OT	BUF.	Norwood 30-yard field goal

ATTENDANCE: 78,389

NOTEWORTHY: *The win was the Bills' 11th of the season. It was only the third team in team history to that point that Buffalo had won at least 11 games (1964, 12; 1980, 11). It was the Jets' first loss in Rich Stadium since 1981. The Bills ran the ball for 229 yards, as Riddick picked up 103 yards (his third and last 100-yard game in his career), and Thurman Thomas supplied 88.*

ONE BILLS DRIVE

AFC PLAYOFFS

JANUARY 1, 1989

OILERS At BILLS

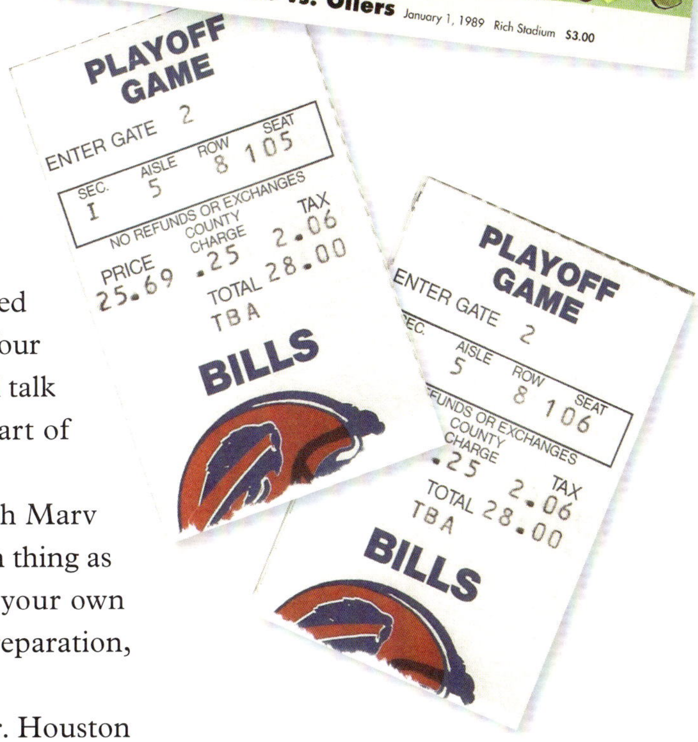

HOME sweet home, at last.

The Buffalo Bills had not hosted a home playoff game since the opening of Rich Stadium in 1973. That was more than 15 years before the playoffs arrived in Orchard Park in January 1989. In addition, the Bills had not played at home for a playoff game since becoming an official member of the National Football League in 1970. The last time the Bills had played a home playoff game was the 1966 AFL championship game played at War Memorial Stadium on January 1, 1967, exactly 32 years prior to the Bills hosting the Houston Oilers.

Buffalo had only played in four playoff games in that 32-year stretch, and each was on the road—at Pittsburgh following the 1974 regular season, 1980 in San Diego, and 1981 at the New York Jets (the lone win), and at Cincinnati.

The home crowd figured to give the Bills a needed boost for the game. The team lost three of its last four regular-season games, quieting some Super Bowl talk that was created by Buffalo's 11–1 run at the start of the season.

"How we finished doesn't matter," head coach Marv Levy said. "This is a new season. There's no such thing as momentum going into the playoffs. You create your own momentum. . . . The most important thing is preparation, not momentum."

The scoreboard was empty in the first quarter. Houston couldn't even record a first down in the opening period. Buffalo had a couple of scoring chances during its possessions. On the first one, Scott Norwood was short on a 50-yard field goal attempt. The second one was set up by a 40-yard run by Thurman Thomas to the Oilers' 12-yard line. But Buffalo could not convert. On fourth and one, Levy went for it, and Kelly's pass to tight end Pete Metzelaars was off the mark.

Leonard Smith blocked a Houston punt early in the second quarter and Buffalo took over at the Oilers' 46. This time, they capitalized. In five plays, Riddick was in the end zone. Houston responded with a field goal. Later in the quarter, Cornelius Bennett blocked an Oilers' 38-yard field goal attempt by Tony Zendejas.

The Bills' special teams had been the difference in the game to that point with two blocked kicks. The night before the matchup, Buffalo special teams coach Bruce DeHaven had given an envelope with single dollar bills in it to his special teams' players. On the back of the bills, DeHaven had written, "Special teams wins championships."

"We heard all week that they had the best special-

Robb Riddick was a short-yardage specialist during his Buffalo career.
CREDIT ROBERT L. SMITH, ORCHARD PARK, NY

teams unit in the NFL," Smith said. "Our special teams rank pretty high also. . . . We have a lot of guys around here with a lot of pride, and we had to show them that our special teams are just as good as any in the league. . . . When it really counted, we were able to come up with a turnover."

The Bills stretched their lead on Thomas's 11-yard touchdown run with less than three minutes left in the third quarter. Buffalo had another chance to tack on a score, following a 53-yard pass from Kelly to Reed, but Riddick was stopped short of the goal line on a fourth-down play to begin the final quarter. Two plays later, Mark Kelso intercepted Warren Moon, and the Bills turned that into a field goal and a 17–3 lead with 11:16 left.

Houston responded with its only touchdown of the game, following an 80-yard drive with Mike Rozier scoring from the 1-yard line. Buffalo received the ensuing kickoff and ran down the clock to the two-minute warning. Houston was ready to get the ball back on a John Kidd punt, but special teamer Steve Tasker forced Curtis Duncan to fumble. Ray Bentley recovered for Buffalo. That ended any hope of an Oilers' comeback. The Bills had secured a 17–10 victory.

"Our guys are hungry," Bennett said. "Our defense is number one in the AFC. You got what you paid to see. This is one of the best defenses in football, and we proved that today."

"Our team played hard against another team that played hard," Levy said. "They played alertly and smart. I've said all along to them, 'Don't be dumb and don't be dirty.' I think we accomplished that. We're going to enjoy it. But I told them, 'Be ready to go back to work tomorrow.'"

Ranked No. 39 of 50 by the authors.

BOX SCORE

	1ST	2ND	3RD	4TH	FINAL
HOUSTON (L)	0	3	0	7	10
BUFFALO (W)	0	7	7	3	17

SCORING SUMMARY:

QTR	TEAM	PLAY
2ND	BUF.	Riddick 1-yard run (Norwood kick)
2ND	HOU.	Zendejas 35-yard field goal
3RD	BUF.	Thomas 11-yard run (Norwood kick)
4TH	BUF.	Norwood 27-yard field goal
4TH	HOU.	Rozier 1-yard run (Zendejas kick)

ATTENDANCE: 79,532

NOTEWORTHY: *Kelly finished the day 19 of 33 for 244 yards with one interception. The 19 completions were a Bills' playoff record. Reed caught six passes for 91 yards. Thomas rushed for 75 yards but on only seven carries. Buffalo gained 372 yards of total offense but missed two fourth-down conversions inside the Oilers' 5-yard line. Buffalo's special teams unit blocked a punt and a field goal and forced a fumble, while holding the Oilers to an average drive start at their own 21-yard line. Darryl Talley led the Bills defense with seven tackles and one sack, and Leonard Smith had six tackles and a blocked punt. Buffalo finished the season undefeated at home with a 9–0 record.*

ONE BILLS DRIVE

OCTOBER 16, 1989

RAMS At BILLS

TIMES WERE TOUGH at One Bills Drive before this game. The Bills were coming off a blowout loss the week before against Indianapolis. Jim Kelly was hurt, and he had made some derogatory comments about his offensive line that did not play well in the locker room. Buffalo was set to start a second-stringer at quarterback against the undefeated Los Angeles Rams. Frank Reich had never started an NFL game in his four-year career and had thrown a total of 40 passes in mop-up duty. Reich had been a third-round draft choice in 1985, and he hadn't given anyone a reason to think that he could be a replacement for Kelly when one was needed.

In other words, there were few reasons for the full house on a Monday night to be very optimistic about the eventual outcome. Little did the fans know that Reich and company had some surprises for them and the Rams.

Buffalo's offense struggled to move the ball in the first half. Reich's first drive under center ended with an interception that set up the only first half touchdown scored by the Rams, an Everett pass. The Bills' next three possessions all ended in three-and-outs. "We had a few problems in the passing game early. It took me a while to get going," Reich said. "But I just said to myself. 'Hang in there, Frank,' I really felt as though we were going to win the game. I just knew it was a question of time before we got things going offensively."

Fortunately for Buffalo, the defense was holding the Rams at bay and set up the first score for the Bills. Defensive end Art Still forced a fumble that was recovered by Jeff Wright at the Rams' 20-yard line. The Bills soon settled for a field goal. Buffalo's second field goal came after a short drive as it took advantage of excellent field position at its own 49-yard line. The Rams got a field goal of their own in the third quarter, and the teams went to the final period with Los Angeles in front 10–6.

Frank Reich throws a pass in his first NFL start at quarterback.
CREDIT ROBERT L. SMITH, ORCHARD PARK, NY

REICH
14

But the lead felt bigger than that and nobody was expecting the fourth quarter fireworks to come. After all, Reich through three quarters had completed only 10 of 24 passes. He was even booed late in the third quarter after a pass he threw hit the ground in front of Thurman Thomas's feet. "I would have booed me too," Reich said. "It was a terrible pass."

The Bills defense had kept them in the game. "Everybody was working as one, and it hadn't been like that all year," nose tackle Fred Smerlas said.

The teams traded field goals early in the fourth quarter, and then Buffalo put together its first sustained drive of the game. Reich directed a 10-play march that ended with a 1-yard touchdown pass to Thomas, and the Bills were ahead for the first time in the game, 16–13.

With the Bills clinging to that three-point advantage and trying to run the clock out, Thomas fumbled at the Rams' 22-yard line with 1:33 left, and LA recovered. On the first play following the fumble, Rams quarterback Jim Everett threw a stunning 78-yard touchdown pass to Willie Anderson. The Rams led 20–16 with only 1:22 remaining. "Frank wasn't rattled at all," tackle Joe Devlin said. "He was determined. You could see it in his eyes that, if we gave him the time and if we executed, he felt like he was going to get it done."

The Bills started from their own 36-yard line and five straight Reich completions later the ball was at the Rams 8-yard line with 20 seconds left. Reed was lined up to Reich's left, and when the ball was snapped, he slanted toward the goal line. Reich fired a bullet into Reed's chest, and the star wide receiver cradled the football as he fell into the end zone for the winning touchdown. *The Buffalo News* columnist Larry Felser described the game "as one of the most stirring victories in Bills history, one of the most unexpected finishes in 20 years of Monday Night Football."

"I was a pretty happy camper . . . and that was really the only way I could express how I felt," said Reich after showing that the Bills weren't necessarily doomed if Kelly was injured. "Those were tears of joy—tears of knowing that, after five years, my prayers were answered. I'm just overjoyed right now, for this team and this organization. And I'm just glad I could be a part of it."

Ranked No. 26 of 50 by the authors.

BOX SCORE

	1ST	2ND	3RD	4TH	FINAL
L.A. RAMS (L, 5-1)	7	0	3	10	20
BUFFALO (W, 4-2)	0	6	0	17	23

SCORING SUMMARY:

QTR	TEAM	PLAY
1ST	LAR.	Everett 3-yard pass to McGee (Lansford kick)
2ND	BUF.	Norwood 38-yard field goal
2ND	BUF.	Norwood 47-yard field goal
3RD	LAR.	Lansford 34-yard field goal
4TH	BUF.	Norwood 40-yard field goal
4TH	LAR.	Lansford 36-yard field goal
4TH	BUF.	Reich 1-yard touchdown pass to Thomas (Norwood kick)
4TH	LAR.	Everett 78-yard pass to Anderson (Lansford kick)
4TH	BUF.	Reich 8-yard pass to Reed (Norwood kick)

ATTENDANCE: 76,231

NOTEWORTHY: *The Bills finished with 348 yards of total offense, but 164 came in the fourth quarter. The defense held the Rams to 266 yards. Everett completed only 15 of 36 passes for 219 yards, but 78 was on one play. And the Bills stuffed the Rams running game, holding LA to 59 yards on 30 carries. Backup linebacker Carlton Bailey was the Bills' unsung hero as he came off the bench after Ray Bentley went out with a head injury and led the team with nine tackles. The Bills unveiled their new $500,000 video scoreboard.*

SEPTEMBER 30, 1990

BRONCOS At BILLS

BILLS general manager Bill Polian only needed one practice to come up with a vivid description of the talents of Cornelius Bennett. He and the Bills had traded for Bennett in the middle of the 1987 season, as the Indianapolis Colts had been unable to reach a contract agreement with the University of Alabama linebacker. Buffalo quickly signed Bennett to a contract and sent him out for a practice.

"I just saw Mickey Mantle in football cleats," Polian exclaimed after the workout.

Mantle was one of the great combinations of speed and power in baseball history. Bennett had those traits as well as he moved into the professional phase of his football career. It took him no time at all to become a great fit into the Bills' defense.

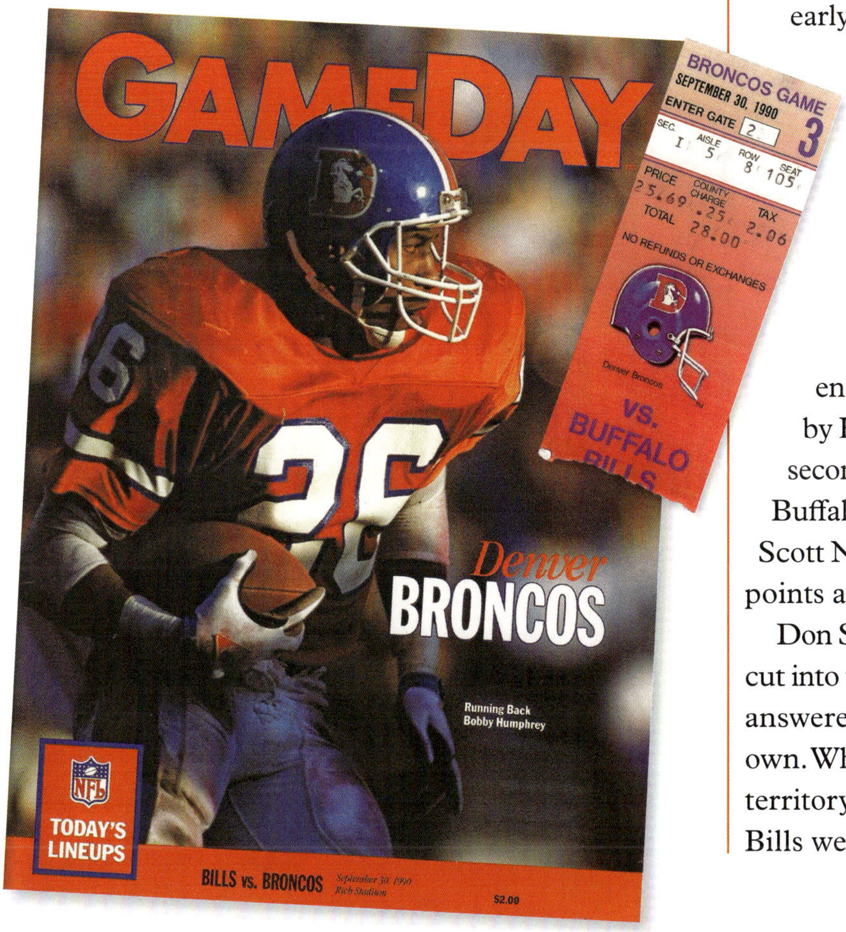

But the linebacker was hampered for part of the 1988 season and all of 1989 with a shoulder injury. It took until 1990 before Bennett was ready to return to his old form. "I feel great," he said in training camp. "As long as I can stay healthy through training camp, people can expect some great things from Cornelius during the season."

Bennett was telling the truth. Ask the Denver Broncos, who were hit by a game-changing hurricane named Bennett during a 1990 visit to Rich Stadium.

This particular matchup had a redemptive feeling to it for the Bills. Denver had come into Buffalo early in the 1989 season and beaten the Bills. If that result had been flipped, Buffalo would have been the AFC's No. 1 seed in the playoffs and the favorite to reach the Super Bowl. But Denver earned both distinctions, and played in the NFL championship game for the third time in four years.

The Broncos started the game well enough, scoring first on a short run by Bobby Humphrey. It was more of the same in the second quarter, as Steve Sewell did the honors. Buffalo's only response came on a field goal by Scott Norwood, and the Bills were behind by 11 points at intermission.

Don Smith's touchdown run in the third quarter cut into that margin, but Denver's Sammy Winder answered it with a short dash for a score of his own. When the Broncos drove deep into Buffalo territory in the fourth quarter, it looked as if the Bills were in deep trouble. At least the Buffalo defense forced a field-goal attempt, but the idea of a 15-point lead with less than 15 minutes to go was daunting.

"We were ready to go up 24–9 and we felt pretty good about the situation," Broncos quarterback John Elway said.

Enter Bennett. David Treadwell's kick was blocked by Nate Odomes, and Bennett caught the ball and had nothing but green artificial turf ahead of him. Eighty yards later, the Bills were back in the game.

"I've been telling Nate he's going to get one," special teams coach Bruce DeHaven said. "He has been coming real close, you know. I said, 'If somebody's just a little bit slow, you're going to get one. It sure as heck came at a good time.'"

On the Broncos' next possession, Elway's pass was deflected at the line of scrimmage by Leon Seals and caught by safety Leonard Smith. He ran through the Denver offense for a touchdown. Suddenly and dramatically, the Bills had taken a 22–21 lead.

"I was still celebrating when I saw Leonard go by me," Seals said. "I said, 'Whoa. Where's that guy going?'"

After the kickoff, Elway fumbled near his own goal line, and Bennett came up with the recovery. Kenneth Davis did the rest on a run on the next play, and the Bills had scored three touchdowns in 77 seconds to take a 29–21 lead.

The Broncos rallied to score a touchdown on a pass by Elway to Ricky Nattiel. If this game was played four years later, Denver could have gone for a two-point conversion to try to tie the game. But that rule wasn't in the books yet, so Treadwell simply added a single point. The Bills recovered the onside kick, and the 29–28 win was theirs.

It wasn't exactly the ideal route toward a victory, but the Bills weren't choosy about their methods as long as they reached the destination.

"I'll tell you what I told our players," Buffalo coach Marv Levy said. "If you don't quit, sometimes you get lucky. I think that prevailed."

As for Bennett, he also had seven tackles, one defended pass, and two near-sacks in which Elway had to throw the ball too soon. Yes, the defender's shoulder was completely healthy again.

"I apologize to the fans for me being injured and not being able to give it my all," he said. "But as long as I stay healthy, you never have to doubt Cornelius Bennett again."

Ranked No. 6 of 50 by the authors.

BOX SCORE

	1ST	2ND	3RD	4TH	FINAL
DENVER (L, 2-2)	7	7	7	7	28
BUFFALO (W, 3-1)	0	3	6	20	29

SCORING SUMMARY:

QTR	TEAM	PLAY
1ST	DEN.	Humphrey 1-yard run (Treadwell kick)
2ND	DEN.	Sewell 3-yard run (Treadwell kick)
2ND	BUF.	Norwood 37-yard field goal
3RD	BUF.	D. Smith 12-yard run
3RD	DEN.	Winder 3-yard run (Treadwell kick)
4TH	BUF.	Bennett 80-yard blocked field goal return (Norwood kick)
4TH	BUF.	Smith 39-yard interception return (kick failed)
4TH	BUF.	Davis 2-yard run (Norwood kick)
4TH	DEN.	Elway 7-yard pass to Nattiel (Treadwell kick)

ATTENDANCE: 74,393

NOTEWORTHY: *Denver had a 410–197 edge in total offense. Elway and Kelly didn't combine for 400 yards passing. Elway was 15 of 28 for 221 yards, while Kelly was 18 of 34 for 167. Humphrey finished with 177 yards rushing on the day. Compare that to the Bills' team total of 64. Denver had a 28–15 edge in first downs. Among those who enjoyed the game was Bills owner Ralph Wilson. "In all my life, I've never seen a game change that rapidly, from almost- certain defeat to a victory."*

Cornelius Bennett played a key role in the Bills' amazing comeback win.

CREDIT ROBERT L. SMITH, ORCHARD PARK, NY

OCTOBER 7, 1990

RAIDERS At BILLS

THE BUFFALO BILLS of the early 1990s were best known for their offense. They had four Hall of Famers on the unit in Jim Kelly, Thurman Thomas, Andre Reed, and James Lofton, and they were working on developing a no-huddle offense that would change the way the game was played. The Bills of 1990 scored 428 points to set a team record . . . only to break it again the following season.

But offenses sometimes can be a little inconsistent. It only takes a tiny mistake to turn a potentially long scoring drive into a three-and-out. Therefore, it helps to have the rest of the roster contribute some big plays at crucial times. The 1990 Bills had that too, especially in the form of a backup wide receiver who became known as one of the greatest special teams' players in NFL history.

Exhibit A for that theory was on display when the Los Angeles Raiders came to Rich Stadium. Los Angeles was 4–0, mostly because of its defense. The Raiders had allowed a total of 35 points in those four games, and the Bills needed to come up with new ways to score to rewrite the script that Los Angeles had used in the season's first month.

There wasn't much drama in the first half of the game, but there was one big play of note. With the Raiders up by a touchdown in the second quarter, the Bills were forced to punt. Tim Brown caught the ball, and was immediately hit by Buffalo's special teams ace, Steve Tasker.

"I was able to get there right as Tim Brown caught it, I wrapped it up, and we twisted around some," Tasker said. "I didn't know the ball came out until I turned around and saw all the guys jumping for something. Then I saw Chris Hale come up with it."

The play led to a touchdown pass from Kelly to Reed that evened the score. Los Angeles took the lead shortly before the half on a field goal. The

Nate Odomes heads for the end zone after a Raiders' fumble.
CREDIT ROBERT L. SMITH, ORCHARD PARK, NY

Raiders made a second-half statement when Marcus Allen scored on a short run to make it a 10-point game. Kelly threw to Keith McKeller for a score to get the Bills back within striking distance, but Schroeder's second touchdown pass put Los Angeles back up by 10. With a 24–14 lead and less than a quarter to go, the Raiders and their strong defense looked to be in a good position.

On the other hand, the Bills were poised for a comeback. "When the clock strikes four [as in fourth quarter], everybody's eyes light up, tails go up, and we just come from under the woodwork," linebacker Darryl Talley said.

The Bills rewrote the script from that point. Kelly's long touchdown pass to Lofton (who had been cut by the Raiders before the 1989 season) reduced the lead to three points and gave the team a shot of adrenaline. Shortly after that, Tasker was untouched as he rushed punter Jeff Gossett.

"They were in a man-for-man blocking scheme and we overloaded the one side," Tasker said. "No one blocked me, and that gave me a clear path to the punter."

After blocking the kick, James Williams scooped up the ball and sprinted 38 yards for a touchdown. Just like that, the Bills had their first lead of the game.

Later in the fourth quarter, Cornelius Bennett forced Schroeder to fumble, and the linebacker even recovered the ball. Scott Norwood gave the Bills a little breathing room with a field goal. The exclamation point came when Nate Odomes stole the ball out of the arms of Willie Gault and went 49 yards for a score. Add it up, and the Bills had scored 24 points in six minutes and three seconds.

What happened? "Well," coach Marv Levy joked, "it is usually my halftime pep talk that does it."

The Bills had a 38–24 win, and they had scored more points in one game than the Raiders had allowed in their first four games.

It was a particularly frustrating outcome for the Raiders, who seemed to be in control for a major portion of the game . . . only to see it slip away under the Bills' avalanche of fourth-quarter points. "They're a pretty good football team," Raiders defensive end Greg Townsend said. "There was a little luck involved, though. . . . They just beat us with fluke plays."

But maybe those plays weren't exactly flukes. After all, Tasker's blocked kick was the fourth of his NFL career. He received a game ball for his efforts—his first such reward in six seasons.

"Hopefully, it won't be the last one," Tasker said. "I'm pretty thrilled about it. This one's going up on the mantle."

Ranked No. 9 of 50 by the authors.

BOX SCORE

	1ST	2ND	3RD	4TH	FINAL
OAKLAND (L, 4-1)	7	3	7	7	24
BUFFALO (W, 4-1)	0	7	7	24	38

SCORING SUMMARY:

QTR	TEAM	PLAY
1ST	OAK.	Schroeder 11-yard pass to Gault (Jaeger kick)
2ND	BUF.	Kelly 13-yard pass to Reed (Norwood kick)
2ND	OAK.	Jaeger 19-yard field goal
3RD	OAK.	Allen 1-yard run (Jaeger kick)
3RD	BUF.	Kelly 15-yard pass to McKeller (Norwood kick)
4TH	OAK.	Schroeder 4-yard pass to Smith (Jaeger kick)
4TH	BUF.	Kelly 42-yard pass to Lofton (Norwood kick)
4TH	BUF.	Williams 38-yard blocked punt return (Norwood kick)
4TH	BUF.	Norwood 23-yard field goal
4TH	BUF.	Odomes 49-yard fumble return (Norwood kick)

ATTENDANCE: 80,076

NOTEWORTHY: *The Bills' offensive totals weren't too inspiring: 14 first downs, 182 passing yards, and only 20 minutes and 46 seconds of possession. But the Raiders had four turnovers, three in the form of fumbles. Schroeder outpassed Kelly with 244 yards in the air. The crowd was the second-largest in Bills history at the time.*

DECEMBER 2, 1990

EAGLES At BILLS

ABOUT 11 MONTHS before this matchup, the Buffalo Bills' offense made an interesting discovery: It was effective when the game's tempo was sped up.

The Bills fell behind Cleveland in a playoff game the previous January, and needed to score points in a hurry. Therefore, Buffalo simply kept lining up without a huddle and winging the ball around Cleveland Stadium. The Bills didn't win the game, but they did come away with the germ of an idea: "What if we did that when we weren't way behind?"

Head coach Marv Levy and offensive coordinator Ted Marchibroda allowed quarterback Jim Kelly to stand in the backfield in the shotgun formation, call the plays, and let 'er rip at times from the start of the 1990 season. The idea proved worthwhile in no time, forcing the Bills to wonder what would happen if they opened a game with it.

When they tried it, they discovered the team could be one of the most awesome offensive forces in football history. The scheme was called the K-Gun, named after tight end Keith McKeller. The idea was that opposing defenses didn't have a chance to catch their collective breaths, let alone substitute fresh players.

The Philadelphia Eagles—on a five-game winning streak entering the game—were the victim of the unveiling. Kelly started the assault with a 63-yard catch-and-run pass to James Lofton for a score just 45 seconds into the game. Scott Norwood added a field goal. Andre Reed caught a 10-yard pass, split the defense, and outran everyone into the end zone for a 56-yard TD. Thurman Thomas caught a short scoring pass, which was set up by another long pass to Lofton. It was 24–0 for Buffalo, and the first quarter wasn't even over yet. The experiment was an unqualified success.

"We kept them in their base [defense] more than they would have liked, I'm sure," Kelly said.

"I had great protection and I was able to find some second and third receivers for big gains."

"My God, it was unbelievable," Eagles coach Buddy Ryan said. "There were people running through the secondary and we couldn't tackle them."

That period went into the history books as a huge milestone in Bills history. Indeed, it's almost as if the rest of the game didn't exist . . . with one big exception. What people don't remember is that the Eagles made a game of it right away. They scored nine quick points, and then Randall Cunningham made a play that will be in the NFL's highlight videos forever.

The Eagles had the ball on their own 5-yard line on third down and 14 with 1:10 left in the first half. After the snap, Cunningham was immediately under siege in the end zone, but somehow avoided three Bills would-be tacklers including Bruce Smith and Cornelius Bennett. He sprinted left to find some open space, and then threw the ball more than 50 yards into a stiff wind. Waiting for the ball was receiver Fred Barnett, who caught the pass and outraced J.D. Williams and Nate Odomes for a touchdown. ESPN's Chris Berman called the second-longest play in Eagles history "the play of the year" that night.

"It was designed," Cunningham said. "I was supposed to drop back, shake to the right. Then Bruce Smith was going to come in and I was supposed to duck. He was supposed to jump over me. I was going to go to Calvin [Williams], but I had to go to Freddy."

Smith had a simple reaction to the play: "I almost had to go change my pants."

When the Eagles scored again in the third quarter on another Cunningham touchdown pass, the Bills' lead was down to 24–23. It looked as if all that memorable work at the game's beginning would become undone. But it was there that most of the scoring stopped.

Norwood kicked a pair of field goals, and that was it for scoreboard alterations. The Bills hung on for a 30–23 win.

"I guess the whole team knew that there were certain individuals in Buffalo who said we weren't going to win any games in December," Kelly said. "We wanted to shove it down a couple of guys' throats, period."

Ranked No. 40 of 50 by the authors.

BOX SCORE

	1ST	2ND	3RD	4TH	FINAL
PHILADELPHIA (L, 7-5)	0	16	7	0	23
BUFFALO (W, 10-2)	24	0	3	3	30

SCORING SUMMARY:

QTR	TEAM	PLAY
1ST	BUF.	Kelly 63-yard pass to Lofton (Norwood kick)
1ST	BUF.	Norwood 43-yard field goal
1ST	BUF.	Kelly 56-yard pass to Reed (Norwood kick)
1ST	BUF.	Kelly 4-yard pass to Thomas (Norwood kick)
2ND	PHI.	Cunningham 18-yard pass to Jackson (kick failed)
2ND	PHI.	Ruzek 32-yard field goal
2ND	PHI.	Cunningham 95-yard pass to Barnett (Ruzek kick)
3RD	PHI.	Cunningham 1-yard pass to Byars (Ruzek kick)
3RD	BUF.	Norwood 21-yard field goal
4TH	BUF.	Norwood 45-yard field goal

ATTENDANCE: 79,320

NOTEWORTHY: *The quarterbacks led the way statistically. Kelly was 19 of 32 for 334 yards. Both Kelly and Cunningham threw their 100th career touchdown pass in the game. Lofton passed Don Maynard and Raymond Berry to move into sixth place in NFL history in all-time receptions with 636. His career total of 11,889 receiving yards ranked third in history, passing Maynard again. Thomas went past the 1,000-yard rushing mark for the second straight season. He became the third Buffalo player to do that (O.J. Simpson and Joe Cribbs.)*

Randall Cunningham of the Eagles tries to run away from superstar Bruce Smith.
CREDIT ROBERT L. SMITH, ORCHARD PARK, NY

34

JANUARY 12, 1991

DOLPHINS At BILLS

THE BUFFALO BILLS had breezed through the 1990 regular season with a 13–3 record. They had rolled up 428 points along the way in compiling the best record in the conference. There was considerable, and justified, talk that this would be the year that the Bills would play in their first-ever Super Bowl.

Buffalo's first playoff opponent in 1991 was only fitting. The Miami Dolphins had handed the Bills their worst loss of the 1990 season—a 30–7 thumping in week two in Miami. The Bills had bounced back to win the rematch at home two days before Christmas, but everyone knew how dangerous the Dolphins were. This would be the first time the two rivals would face each other in the postseason, and the game was in Rich Stadium, where the Bills had beaten the Dolphins in four straight games.

If that weren't enough to stir everyone up, the quarterback matchup was out of a dream. The Bills' Jim Kelly and the Dolphins' Dan Marino were well into careers that would put them in the Pro Football Hall of Fame. Kelly was back in the lineup after missing the final two weeks of the regular season with an injured knee. Now they'd square off on a day where defenders were having a tough time keeping their footing because of a little snow. Footballs figured to be flying around Rich Stadium on a Saturday afternoon in January.

That they were. Kelly and Marino led their respective teams into a shootout that left almost everyone breathless.

The first quarter set the tone. Kelly hit Andre Reed with a medium-length pass, and he split the Miami defense on his way to a touchdown. Miami responded with a field goal, but Buffalo's Scott Norwood kicked a pair of three-pointers of his own to give the Bills a 10-point lead. And when Thurman Thomas ran five yards for a score in the second period, the Bills were up 20–3. Yes, the weather seemed to be a factor . . . for the Dolphins.

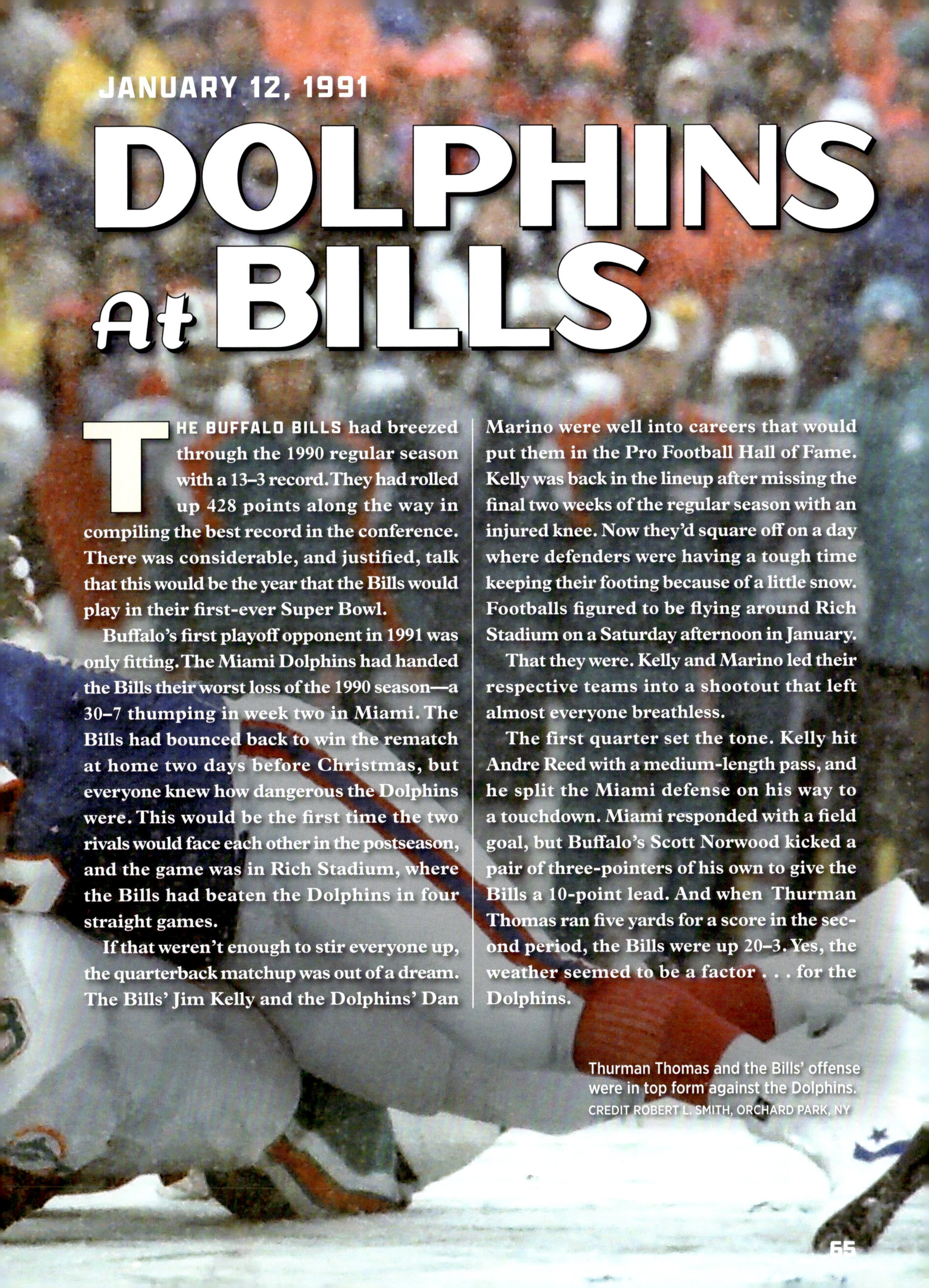

Thurman Thomas and the Bills' offense were in top form against the Dolphins.
CREDIT ROBERT L. SMITH, ORCHARD PARK, NY

"We were slippin' and slidin' out there," Miami cornerback J.B. Brown said. "It baffled me. They didn't slip at all, and we couldn't stand up."

That meant Marino was going to have to throw a lot if he had hopes of rallying his team to a win.

That's what he did, starting with a long scoring pass to Mark Duper. The Bills answered with a scoring pass from Kelly to James Lofton, who did some high stepping while cruising into the end zone, but Marino scampered two yards late in the first half to make it 27–17. The Bills were on a 54-point pace at that point, but no one felt completely secure about the outcome.

The teams traded field goals in the third period to maintain the 10-point margin. At the start of the fourth quarter, Marino had a touchdown flip to offensive tackle Roy Foster—who awkwardly celebrated the only touchdown in his two-year career—to cut the lead to 30–27. In other words, anyone's game.

But the Bills responded like champions. They scored two touchdowns in short order, including another good-sized pass to Reed. "They went right down the field and scored. Your heart drops right into your stomach," Dolphins receiver Jim Jensen said.

At 44–27, the Dolphins weren't coming back. Marino tried his best, and he did throw one more touchdown pass. That was it. The Bills had too many weapons in a 44–34 victory. The game set an NFL record for most points in a playoff game that ended in regulation time. San Diego and Miami ran up 79 points in a double-overtime game in 1981.

Buffalo ran a no-huddle offense for most of the game, and the team's wide receivers were the stars. Lofton caught seven passes for 149 yards, while Reed had four catches for 122 yards.

"In every playoff game I've been in so far, I've had the fortune to play fairly well," Lofton said. "You just play. And if they come to you with the ball, you try and make the plays."

With the Dolphins sent home for the season, there was one more obstacle that the Bills needed to clear in order to reach their first Super Bowl: The Los Angeles Raiders.

"We were the two division winners with the best records, so maybe it's appropriate we do face each other," Levy said.

Ranked No. 13 of 50 by the authors.

BOX SCORE

	1ST	2ND	3RD	4TH	FINAL
MIAMI (L)	3	14	3	14	34
BUFFALO (W)	13	14	3	14	44

SCORING SUMMARY:

QTR	TEAM	PLAY
1ST	BUF.	Kelly 40-yard pass to Reed (Norwood kick)
1ST	MIA.	Stoyanovich 49-yard field goal
1ST	BUF.	Norwood 24-yard field goal
1ST	BUF.	Norwood 22-yard field goal
2ND	BUF.	Thomas 5-yard run (Norwood kick)
2ND	MIA.	Marino 64-yard pass to Duper (Stoyanovich kick)
2ND	BUF.	Kelly 13-yard pass to Lofton (Norwood kick)
2ND	MIA.	Marino 2-yard run (Stoyanovich kick)
3RD	MIA.	Stoyanovich 22-yard field goal
3RD	BUF.	Norwood 28-yard field goal
4TH	MIA.	Marino 2-yard pass to Foster (Stoyanovich kick)
4TH	BUF.	Thomas 5-yard run (Norwood kick)
4TH	BUF.	Kelly 26-yard pass to Reed (Norwood kick)
4TH	MIA.	Marino 8-yard pass to Martin (Stoanovich kick)

ATTENDANCE: 77,087

NOTEWORTHY: *Kelly was an effective 19 of 29 for 339 yards with only one interception, while, Marino was 23 of 49 for 323 yards and three touchdowns with two interceptions. Thomas ran for 117 yards on 32 carries, supplying necessary balance to Buffalo's attack. Both teams finished with 24 first downs.*

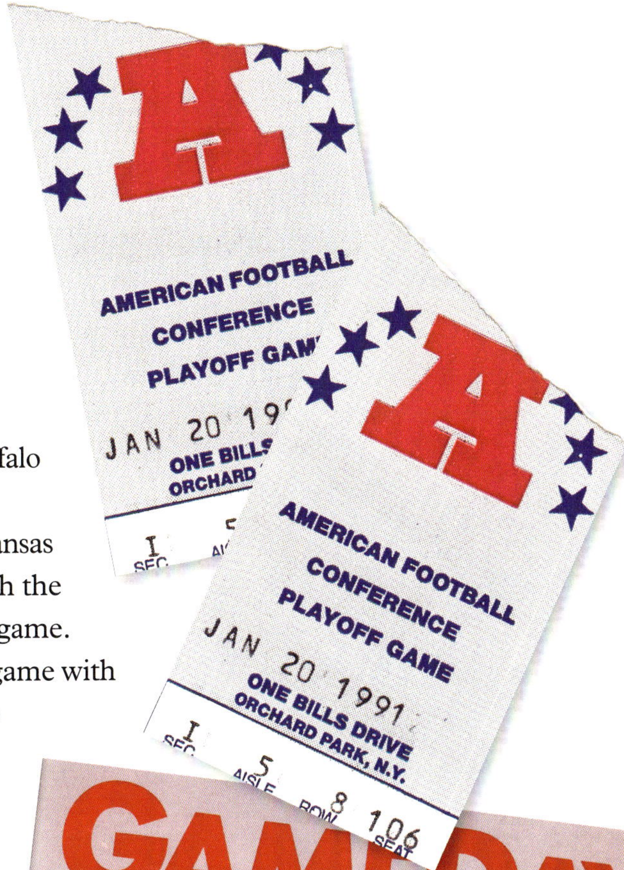

JANUARY 20, 1991

RAIDERS At BILLS

THIS WAS the biggest home game for the Buffalo Bills in a generation.

On January 1, 1967, the Bills played the Kansas City Chiefs in War Memorial Stadium, with the winner advancing to the first NFL–AFL championship game. Buffalo lost the game 31–7, and hadn't played a home game with the chance to reach a Super Bowl for more than two decades after that. The Bills' only opportunity to reach the title contest came in January 1989, when they lost the AFC Championship Game in Cincinnati.

Now opportunity truly knocked. The Bills hosted the Los Angeles Raiders in Rich Stadium with their best chance yet to reach their first Super Bowl. If they needed motivation, they only needed to look at their recent history. Buffalo had lost playoff games in the previous two years, falling short of its goal.

The Raiders (12–4) were one of the winningest franchises in the NFL for the previous three decades, and they brought a swagger with them that emanated from the top of the organization with owner Al Davis. They had won 13 Western Division titles in the previous 24 years, were appearing in their 11th AFC Championship game, and had three Super Bowl victories to their credit However, none of those titles had come since 1985.

"They have a number of players who have been a lot further than us," Bruce Smith said. "They have an advantage, and the fact we made the playoffs the last two years does not make a difference. But it's a known fact we've not been able to do it when it counted, and it counts now. It

isn't promised to us next year we will get this far. So we have to take care of it now."

Buffalo wasted absolutely no time in showing it was ready to fulfill the team's promise.

Jim Kelly ran off five plays in rapid succession that gained 12, 14, 15, 9, and 5 yards to the Raiders' 20-yard line. Los Angeles defensive end Howie Long was so tired already that he signaled for a timeout to catch his breath—five plays into the game. Four plays later, the Bills were on the scoreboard as Kelly—after fumbling the snap—recovered and found James Lofton alone in the end zone.

"I really think they weren't prepared for it," Thurman Thomas said about the Buffalo offense.

"We've been running it for a long time now, and you would think the [Raiders] coaches would know that's what got us this far and would prepare for it."

The Raiders answered with a field goal, which would be their only response of the day. Four plays later, the Bills were in the end zone again on a Thomas run. Before the first quarter ended, the teams traded interceptions, but Jay Schroeder's interception was returned by Bills linebacker Darryl Talley for a touchdown. Buffalo had a 21–3 lead before the end of the quarter. "The first thing I thought was, 'The football's coming,'" Talley said. "And as soon as I got the ball, the only thing I could think of was to get to the end zone as fast as I could."

Buffalo's dominance continued in the second quarter. Kenneth Davis scored twice on short runs, and Lofton caught his second touchdown pass of the game. The Bills led 41–3 at halftime. It was an NFL record for points in a half. There was little doubt that the Bills were on their way to the first Super Bowl appearance in team history. It was only a question of what the final score would be.

The 80,324 fans—the largest crowd in Rich Stadium history—spent the entire second half partying and counting down the minutes. Buffalo scored 10 more points after the break as Davis scored his third touchdown, and Scott Norwood kicked a field goal to make the final score 51–3, the biggest rout in AFC Championship game history.

BOX SCORE

	1ST	2ND	3RD	4TH	FINAL
L.A. RAIDERS (L)	3	0	0	0	3
BUFFALO (W)	21	20	0	10	51

SCORING SUMMARY:

QTR	TEAM	PLAY
1ST	BUF.	Kelly 13-yard pass to Lofton (Norwood kick)
1ST	LAR.	Jaeger 41-yard field goal
1ST	BUF.	Thomas 12-yard run (Norwood kick)
1ST	BUF.	Talley 27-yard interception return (Norwood kick)
2ND	BUF.	Davis 1-yard run (kick blocked)
2ND	BUF.	Davis 3-yard run (Norwood kick)
2ND	BUF.	Kelly 8-yard pass to Lofton (Norwood kick)
4TH	BUF.	Davis 1-yard run (Norwood kick)
4TH	BUF.	Norwood 39-yard field goal

ATTENDANCE: 80,324

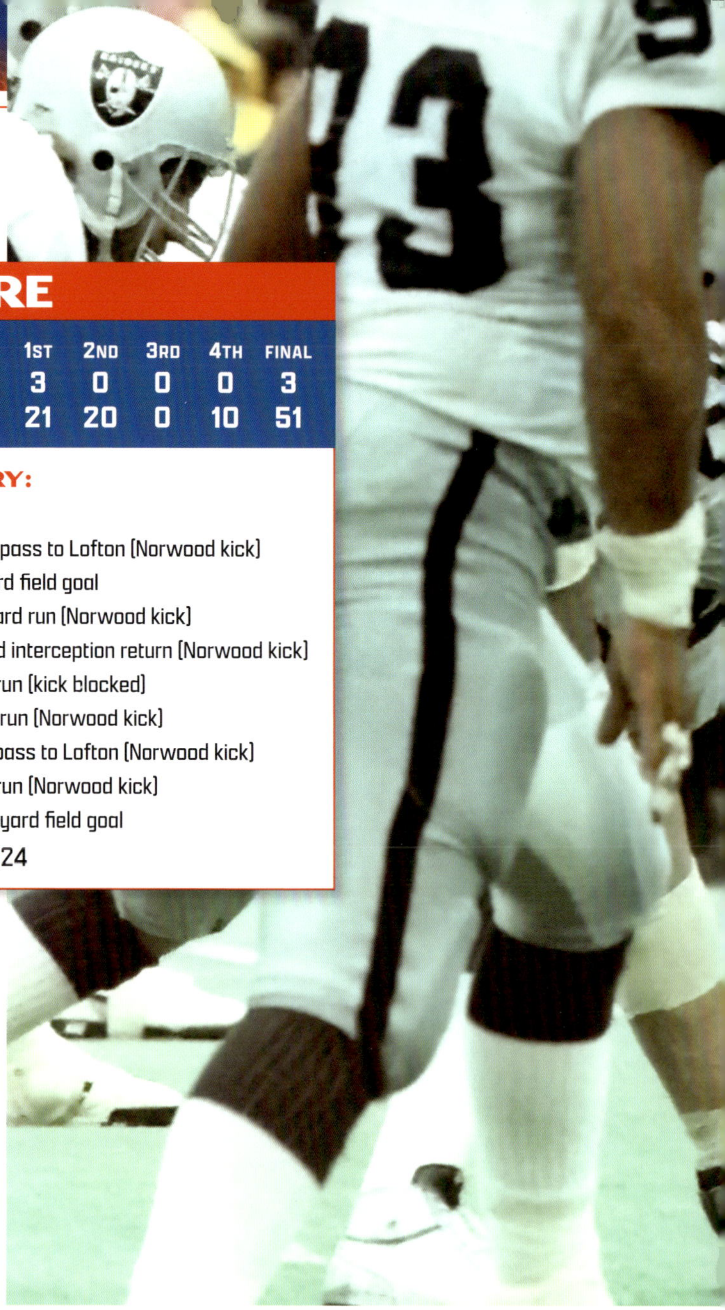

The Bills' offense was unstoppable in advancing to Buffalo's first Super Bowl.
CREDIT ROBERT L. SMITH, ORCHARD PARK, NY

It was the greatest performance by a Bills team in franchise history then, and it still stands as that today. Buffalo left no doubt who was the best team in the AFC in 1990; now it had the challenge of winning the franchise's first Super Bowl.

"Everybody's saying, 'We're going to the Super Bowl," Kelly said. "But my goal isn't to go to the Super Bowl. My goal is to win it. A lot of teams get the chance, but 20 years down the road, I don't want people to say, 'Oh Buffalo was in it, BUT . . . 'We have one more river to cross."

Ranked No. 2 of 50 by the authors.

NOTEWORTHY: *Kelly completed 17 of 23 passes for 300 yards and two touchdowns with one interception. Thomas rushed for 138 yards on 25 carries while Davis only ran for 21 yards, but his three rushing touchdowns set an AFC championship game record that he still holds with three other players. Buffalo amassed 502 yards of total offense and 30 first downs. The Bills defense also played well, completely shutting down the Raiders' passing offense. L.A.'s two quarterbacks, Schroeder and Vince Evans, completed 15 of 39 passes for 176 yards with six interceptions. The official no-show count for the game was 38.*

ONE BILLS DRIVE

SEPTEMBER 1, 1991

DOLPHINS At BILLS

THE BILLS OPENED their 1991 season with the Miami Dolphins coming to Rich Stadium. Could anyone in Buffalo have asked for a better way to start the football year?

The Bills–Dolphins rivalry had some history behind it. Miami had dominated the matchup for many years, but the arrival of future Hall of Famers Jim Kelly, Marv Levy, and Bill Polian caused the relationship to become far less one-sided. From 1988 through 1990, the Bills had beaten the Dolphins in six of seven games—including a playoff offensive shootout that pushed Buffalo toward its first Super Bowl in January 1991.

"We're so competitive with Buffalo," Miami coach Don Shula said. "After losing the playoff game up there and then knowing we would open with them, that really gave our offseason a lot of purpose and our training camp a lot of purpose."

Even better was the fact that games involving Buffalo and Miami usually were extremely entertaining, mostly because of the quarterbacks. Kelly and Dan Marino of the Dolphins were both capable of putting points on the scoreboard in a hurry. And so they did.

The game did not start well for the home team. Scott Norwood missed a 25-yard field goal on the Bills' first possession. Four plays later, Marino passed to Mark Clayton for the game's first score. On Buffalo's next possession, defensive back Louis Oliver intercepted Jim Kelly at the Miami 2-yard line. The Dolphins eventually converted that into a short touchdown run.

The Bills stopped making mistakes at that point. Kelly hit Andre Reed with a 54-yard scoring strike, cutting Miami's lead to 14–7 before halftime. The Dolphins played an efficient first half, taking advantage of a Bills' defense that was missing 1990 Defensive Player of the Year Bruce Smith due to injury.

Andre Reed takes off after one of his 11 receptions.
CREDIT ROBERT L. SMITH, ORCHARD PARK, NY

"At halftime I was just sitting at my locker by myself; the rest of the offensive players and coaches were on the other side," Thurman Thomas said. "I think they knew I was kinda mad. I didn't say anything to anyone. I knew they knew when I touched the ball a lot against the Dolphins, we usually won. So, I figured I'd get it more in the second half. At least I hoped so."

Miami extended its lead early in the third quarter with a short field goal. The Bills responded, but not before losing Kelly with an ankle injury. "The biggest thing that scared us was going down inside the 20 twice and coming away with no points," Bills center Kent Hull said. "That was scary, and then Jim went down and there was a lot of things that were starting to happen, and we thought, 'Oh God, here we go, we're falling apart.' But we came back." Backup quarterback Frank Reich finished the drive with a short touchdown pass to Butch Rolle.

After it was announced in the press box that he would not return, Kelly was back on the field the next time the Bills had the ball. "It's going to take a lot more than a bum ankle to keep me out," he said. "If I can take the field, this is my club. I'm going to do it."

He certainly shook off the injury quickly as he hit James Lofton on a 27-yard pass. Then Kelly threw 23 yards to Thomas, and the running back carried the ball the final 27 yards for a 50-yard touchdown. The Bills were in the lead for the first time, 21–17. Marino put the Dolphins back in front early in the fourth quarter on a short pass for a touchdown to Clayton. Not to be outdone, Kelly quickly moved Buffalo down the field and Carwell Gardner lugged the ball the final yard. Buffalo was back in front, 28–24.

Later, Miami faced a third and one at its own 47-yard line with 6:52 left, when Ray Bentley made the play of the game. The Bills linebacker knocked the ball loose from Higgs and Mark Kelso recovered. "That was the key to the game," Hull said.

Less than three minutes later, Thomas ran the final seven yards for a touchdown to push Buffalo's lead to 11. Miami scored a late touchdown, but the Bills then ran out the clock for the come-from-behind 35–31 victory. Whew.

"When we were coming off the field, Dan Marino walked up to me and said, 'Hopefully, you'll see us a few more times this season,'" Kelly said. "I told him, 'That would be fine with me.'"

Ranked No. 33 of 50 by the authors.

BOX SCORE

	1ST	2ND	3RD	4TH	FINAL
MIAMI (L, 0-1)	7	7	3	14	31
BUFFALO (W, 1-0)	0	7	14	14	35

SCORING SUMMARY:

QTR	TEAM	PLAY
1st	MIA.	Marino 43-yard pass to Clayton (Baumann kick)
2nd	MIA.	Higgs 3-yard run (Baumann kick)
2nd	BUF.	Kelly 54-yard pass to Reed (Norwood kick)
3rd	MIA.	Baumann 21-yard field goal
3rd	BUF.	Reich 3-yard pass to Rolle (Nowood kick)
3rd	BUF.	Kelly 50-yard pass to Thomas (Norwood kick)
4th	MIA.	Marino 5-yard pass to Clayton (Baumann kick)
4th	BUF.	Gardner 1-yard run (Norwood kick)
4th	BUF.	Thomas 7-yard run (Norwood kick)

ATTENDANCE: 80,252

NOTEWORTHY: *The Bills set a team record for total yards in a single game with 583, breaking the record of 564 in a 1964 game against Houston. Thomas became the first player in Bills history to have both 100 yards rushing and receiving in the same game (165 rushing yards on 25 carries and 103 receiving yards on eight catches). Reed had 11 receptions for 154 yards, and he and Thomas became the first Bills duo to have 100 yards receiving in the same game since 1970.*

SEPTEMBER 8, 1991

STEELERS At BILLS

DON BEEBE may have been a "third" wide receiver for the Bills during their glory days of the 1990s, but he certainly came up with some valuable contributions along the way. This particular day might have been as good as any of them on a personal level.

After all, not too many players catch four touchdown passes in a single game.

After grabbing No. 4 on a memorable day against the Pittsburgh Steelers, wide receiver Don Beebe and quarterback Jim Kelly had a spirited conversation on the sidelines.

"I was telling him that I wanted my $400," Beebe said with a smile. "He gives $100 to each of his receivers who catches a touchdown pass."

It was a good investment by Kelly. Beebe went on to play nine years in the NFL, six with the Bills. But this was his best year in terms of touchdown catches with six, sparked by this memorable performance.

After a missed field goal on their first possession, the Kelly-led offense scored the next four times it had the football. It took two plays for Buffalo to score its first touchdown on a 47-yard pass that James Lofton caught at the Steelers' 6-yard line and sprinted into the end zone to cap off the 62-yard drive. Norwood made a 50-yard field goal attempt, the longest of his career to that point, that extended the Bills lead to 10–0.

After a Steelers' field goal, two Kelly-to-Beebe touchdown passes put the Bills in the lead 24–3. "That Beebe," marveled Pittsburgh All-Pro cornerback Rod Woodson. "or whatever his name is, he looked like he was a Hall of Famer."

Kelly completed 18 of 24 passes for 240 yards and three touchdowns in the first half. That would

FJ
44

normally be considered an excellent game for a quarterback. And Kelly was only getting started. "I think Jim Kelly played a magnificent game," Bills head coach Marv Levy said. "I think if you're going to throw the ball and rely heavily on what our approach to offense is, you're not going to play interception-less football. He played a great game, no buts about it."

On the first drive of the second half, the East Brady, Pennsylvania, star directed an 80-yard march that was finished off with his touchdown pass to Andre Reed. Trailing by 31–10, Pittsburgh answered with three consecutive scores that included an interception return by linebacker Bryan Hinkle of an errant Kelly pass for a touchdown. At that point, the Steelers only trailed 31–27.

But on this day, the Kelly-to-Beebe combination was unstoppable. The two hooked up for two more touchdowns and Nate Odomes's pick-six was mixed in as the Bills went on to a 52–34 victory. It was the second-most points the Bills had ever scored in a game.

"I ran out of plays," Kelly said. "It got to a point where it was, 'What do I call now?' We ran so many variations on our plays, we ran everything three or four times." Beebe had a career day with 10 catches for 112 yards and four touchdowns. Reed did not have a bad day either with nine receptions for 118 yards and one score, while James Lofton reeled in four passes for 78 more yards and a touchdown.

"I would hate to play defense against us," Beebe said. "Running patterns, you can just see in the DB's eyes, it's like 'Who's coming next?' I don't know how (anyone) can stop it."

"There's not much to say when we get it handed to us the way we did today," Steelers head coach Chuck Noll said. "We had some opportunities and we couldn't take advantage of them, but Buffalo just played exceptionally well, very, very well."

Pittsburgh cornerback Woodson added, "They made us look like little kids out there."

Ranked No. 36 of 50 by the authors.

BOX SCORE

	1ST	2ND	3RD	4TH	FINAL
PITTSBURGH (L, 1-1)	0	10	17	7	34
BUFFALO (W, 2-0)	10	14	7	21	52

SCORING SUMMARY:

QTR	TEAM	PLAY
1ST	BUF.	Kelly 53-yard pass to Lofton (Norwood kick)
1ST	BUF.	Norwood 50-yard field goal
2ND	PIT.	Anderson 25-yard field goal
2ND	BUF.	Kelly 34-yard pass to Beebe (Norwood kick)
2ND	BUF.	Kelly 14-yard pass to Beebe (Norwood kick)
2ND	PIT.	Foster 56-yard run (Anderson kick)
3RD	BUF.	Kelly 14-yard pass to Reed (Norwood kick)
3RD	PIT.	Williams 1-yard run (Anderson kick)
3RD	PIT.	Hinkle 57-yard interception return (Anderson kick)
3RD	PIT.	Anderson 27-yard field goal
4TH	BUF.	Kelly 11-yard pass to Beebe (Norwood kick)
4TH	BUF.	Kelly 4-yard pass to Beebe (Norwood kick)
4TH	BUF.	Odomes 32-yard interception return (Norwood kick)
4TH	PIT.	Hoge 1-yard run (Anderson kick)

ATTENDANCE: 79,545

NOTEWORTHY: *Kelly completed 31 of 43 passes for 363 yards. His six touchdown passes set a Bills team record that still stands today. The Bills also rushed for 194 yards, and the team's total offense was 537 yards. They converted 31 first downs. Thurman Thomas quietly rushed for 107 yards on 15 carries. Scott Norwood and Pete Metzelaars played in their 100th game as Buffalo Bills. Beebe's four touchdown receptions in a single game tied a Bills record held by former Bill Jerry Butler. The best sign at Rich Stadium said, "Welcome to Buffalo's Palace of Points." It was the Bills' 12th consecutive victory at home, a streak that would reach 17 before the Bills lost a meaningless end-of-season game without many of their starters playing.*

Don Beebe has one of his four end-zone celebrations in the game with the Steelers.
CREDIT ROBERT L. SMITH, ORCHARD PARK, NY

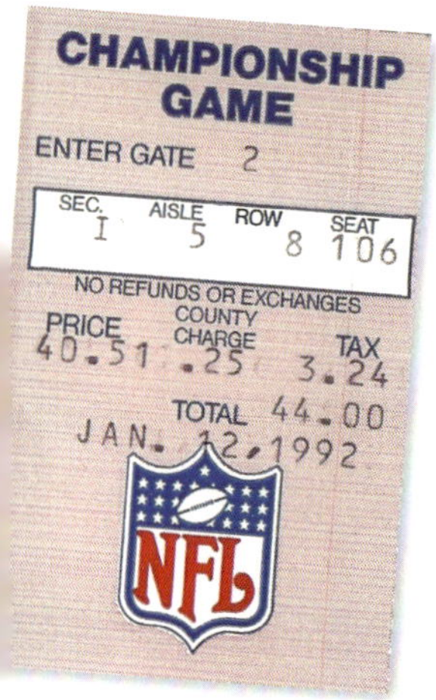

JANUARY 12, 1992

BRONCOS At BILLS

IT'S NOT EASY to return to the Super Bowl after losing.

When the Bills took the field on this particular January day in 1992, only four teams had ever done it. In 1972, Dallas rebounded from a loss to win the Super Bowl, and Miami did the same a year later. Minnesota made it two straight losses in the title game in 1975, and Denver did the same in 1988.

A return had been the Bills' goal throughout the 1991 season. They probably had the better team in the previous Super Bowl, but lost by a whisker to the New York Giants. Now Buffalo was one win away from heading back to the title game and its accompanying second chance.

"We're this close to getting back and getting a bigger taste of what we felt last year," Bills center Kent Hull said. "This football team is not screaming and jumping and turning flips about it. It's approaching things in a very businessman-like manner."

The stars of the AFC Championship game were the two quarterbacks. John Elway of the Broncos and Jim Kelly of the Bills proved to be as good as advertised during their careers. They were both taken in the famous 1983 draft, which also featured Dan Marino of the Dolphins. All three ended up in the Pro Football Hall of Fame. Elway and Kelly seemed capable of leading their respective teams to points. The idea, from a defensive standpoint, was not to let them.

"You see Kelly beating a lot of people deep," said Broncos defensive coordinator and future Bills head coach Wade Phillips to *Sports Illustrated*. "But we're not going to get beat deep, not with

Carlton Bailey scored the lone touchdown of his career when it mattered most.
CREDIT ROBERT L. SMITH, ORCHARD PARK, NY

Linebacker Cornelius Bennett wraps up a Broncos running back during the AFC championship game.
CREDIT GETTY IMAGES

the zone we play. We might get beat underneath, but not deep."

The two quarterbacks and their teams could do nothing in the first 30 minutes. They combined for zero points, which is very unusual for any NFL game—let alone one in the conference title matchup. There hadn't been a 0–0 first half in an AFC championship game since 1983, when the New York Jets and Miami Dolphins couldn't score. As a *Sports Illustrated* writer wrote later, a Shootout became a Shutout.

The Bills' possessions in the first half ended

punt, punt, interception, punt, punt, punt, halftime. Then again, Denver didn't do much better. "Our defense is becoming a monster," Bills defensive line coach Chuck Dickerson characteristically said in his colorful way. "I was having a hard time getting the slobber off my chin, I was so excited watching them."

After 40 minutes of play, the score was still 0–0 and people started to wonder if the first score would ever come. "By about then I thought 3–0 would win it," Phillips said.

Finally, someone did carry the football over the goal line in the third quarter. However, the person who scored was a surprise to everyone. The play started when Elway tried to throw a screen pass to Steve Sewell. Nose tackle Jeff Wright made the most famous play of his career, tipping the ball up in the air. Linebacker Carlton Bailey of the Bills caught it and rumbled 11 yards for the opening touchdown in the biggest play of *his* career.

It was the second and last interception of Bailey's 10-year career in the NFL, and the only time he ever scored any points on the field. Bailey wasn't exactly used to scoring, even going back to his beginnings. "In high school, I just blocked," Bailey said. "It couldn't come at a better time."

The Bills added a field goal by Scott Norwood with 4:18 left in the fourth quarter. Even better from a Bills' standpoint, Elway had been replaced by Gary Kubiak by that point. The superstar suffered an injured thigh and limped off the field in the fourth quarter with his day completed. The new quarterback for Denver did his best under difficult circumstances. He finished the game 11 of 12 for 136 yards. Kubiak put the Broncos on the scoreboard with a short run to narrow the lead to 10–7.

But that was as close as Denver could get. The Broncos' last hope ended when Sewell fumbled with 1:28 left. Kirby Jackson of Buffalo recovered the loose football. The Bills ran out the clock from there. They were headed to Super Bowl No. 2.

"That's what a championship game is supposed to be like," Kelly said. "All during the course of the week, you heard about Elway, Kelly and the whole offense and didn't hear much about either defense."

The "what ifs?" in a game like that were many. Denver had 14 possessions, and reached Bills' territory on 10 of them. They scored once. Kicker David Treadwell of the Broncos missed three field goals. Two hit the upright and bounced harmlessly away.

No matter. The Bills had achieved their goal of reaching another Super Bowl. Now came the tough part.

"We have one more river to cross," General Manager Bill Polian said.

Ranked No. 14 of 50 by the authors.

BOX SCORE

	1ST	2ND	3RD	4TH	FINAL
DENVER (L)	0	0	0	7	7
BUFFALO (W)	0	0	7	3	10

SCORING SUMMARY:

QTR	TEAM	PLAY
3RD	BUF.	Bailey 11-yard interception return (Norwood kick)
4TH	BUF.	Norwood 44-yard field goal
4TH	DEN.	Kubiak 3-yard run (Treadwell kick)

ATTENDANCE: 80,272

NOTEWORTHY: *Kelly finished the day 13 of 25 for 117 yards, with his longest pass of the day a 25-yarder to Keith McKeller. Thurman Thomas ground out 72 yards on 26 carries. Buffalo lost the total yardage battle, 304 to 213. Both teams had two turnovers. It was Denver's first-ever loss in the AFC Championship game after four wins.*

JANUARY 3, 1993

OILERS At BILLS

ASK MOST Buffalo Bills' fans what was the best game ever played in the team's history at the original stadium in Orchard Park, and most probably would answer by saying "The Comeback." No other words are necessary.

Yet it was a game in which many fans headed for the exits early in order to beat the traffic—as early as the third quarter. It would be interesting to know how many admit to that error in judgment even today. On the other hand, the cause did look lost, and the season looked over. Could you blame them?

Optimism was not in great supply as the Bills prepared for their playoff opener against the Houston Oilers. The reasons were many, but the biggest was injuries. Jim Kelly had sprained his ankle in the finale to the regular season, a 27–3 romp by these same Oilers. He was ruled out of the rematch. Frank Reich was a very good reserve quarterback, but no team wants to be missing the starter at that key position at playoff time. Besides, Frank had no playoff experience. Still, Reich accepted the challenge.

"It seems that over my career, each situation I've been in has been stepped up a level higher. . . . I'm terribly excited," he said. "It can't get here soon enough as far as I'm concerned."

Buffalo's hopes seemed to shrink by the minute during the course of the first half. Houston's famous "run and shoot" offense was in top form for the first 30 minutes. The Oilers warmed up in the first quarter with a short touchdown pass from Warren Moon to Haywood Jeffires.

The second period turned into the Bills' worst nightmare. After three more scores, Houston went into intermission with a stunning 28–3 lead.

It became even worse early in the second half. Reich's sideline pass was intercepted by Houston's Bubba McDowell, who had clear sailing for a touchdown and a 35–3 lead. The Bills' hopes

BOX SCORE

	1ST	2ND	3RD	4TH	OT	FINAL
HOUSTON (L)	7	21	7	3	0	38
BUFFALO (W)	3	0	28	7	3	41

SCORING SUMMARY:

QTR	TEAM	PLAY
1ST	HOU.	Moon 3-yard pass to Jeffires (Del Greco kick)
1ST	BUF.	Christie 36-yard field goal
2ND	HOU.	Moon 7-yard pass to Slaughter (Del Greco kick)
2ND	HOU.	Moon 26-yard pass to Duncan (Del Greco kick)
2ND	HOU.	Moon 27-yard pass to Jeffires (Del Greco kick)
3RD	HOU.	McDowell 58-yard interception return (Del Greco kick)
3RD	BUF.	Davis 1-yard run (Christie kick)
3RD	BUF.	Reich 38-yard pass to Beebe (Christie kick)
3RD	BUF.	Reich 26-yard pass to Reed (Christie kick)
3RD	BUF.	Reich 18-yard pass to Reed (Christie kick)
4TH	BUF.	Reich 17-yard pass to Reed (Christie kick)
4TH	HOU.	Del Greco 26-yard field goal
OT	BUF.	Christie 32-yard field goal

ATTENDANCE: 75,141

seemed dead. Even Marv Levy was convinced of that. When asked about what he thought about his team's chances when down by 32, he replied, "About the same chance you have of winning the New York State Lottery."

Kenneth Davis finally put a touchdown on the scoreboard with a short run for the Bills, who soon edged closer when Reich completed a 38-yard touchdown pass to Don Beebe. Steve Christie supplied another boost when he mis-hit an onside kick, only to recover the ball himself. Reich capitalized on the play quickly with a pass to Andre Reed, who sort of stumbled in for a score. Suddenly it was 35–24.

Andre Reed heads for the end zone in the game known as "The Comeback."
CREDIT ROBERT L. SMITH, ORCHARD PARK, NY

Buffalo wasn't done scoring in the third quarter. Reich and Reed teamed up again on another big touchdown pass, their third such combination in the period. Reed dove, caught the fourth-down pass, and slid into the end zone. The Bills only trailed by 35–31, and a quarter of the game remained. After the Bills scored four touchdowns in less than seven minutes, anything was now possible.

The Bills completed the rally when Reich and Reed combined for yet another score when the receiver split the defense to be open in the end zone. With 3:08 left, Buffalo had taken the lead.

Bills' radio announcer Van Miller said on the air at that point, "It is bedlam here at Rich. It is fan-demoniom. It is pandemonium. It is fantastic."

But the Oilers weren't dead yet. Moon led Houston down the field again, as the offense suddenly returned to its first-half form. Buffalo was lucky that the Oilers had to settle for a field goal to send the contest to overtime.

Houston won the coin toss, and it was easy to wonder if it would continue to move the ball. Bills cornerback Nate Odomes had other ideas. On the Oilers' third play in overtime, Moon threw the ball almost directly to Odomes, who intercepted it.

Christie, almost automatic in such situations, soon ended the drama with a 32-yard field goal. The greatest comeback in NFL history resulted in a 41–38 Bills win. It was a great way for Christie to end his first-ever playoff game. "Wow! Are all playoff games like this?" he asked.

"If there had been a breakdown in any point in our football team, we wouldn't have won the football game," center Kent Hull said. "It took almost perfect execution by all 45 players in the second half to win, and that's what happened."

All of that combined to create a spectacular game. But its description also buries the most important part of the story. The Bills were still alive in the playoffs, and they still had hopes of reaching a third straight Super Bowl. It wouldn't be easy, since the team would hit the road for any future playoff games, but it was possible. They couldn't have asked for more, especially at halftime.

Ranked No. 1 of 50 by the authors.

NOTEWORTHY: *The teams combined for 79 points, tying the NFL playoff record at the time. The eight combined touchdown passes in the game set a league playoff record. The Bills improved to 6–0 in playoff games held at Rich Stadium.*

ONE BILLS DRIVE

DECEMBER 26, 1993

JETS At BILLS

EVER TRY TO kick a football in temperatures approaching zero degrees? Give it a try sometime, and you'll find that it's about as much fun as kicking a football-sized rock.

Then do it in a pressure situation, and you'll see what Cary Blanchard experienced near the end of this game between the Bills and Jets.

The temperature that day was a frosty 9 degrees, with a wind chill of -28. The area had received 20 inches of snow on Christmas Eve, and temporary workers were hired to come in the next day and get the stadium ready for play. Bills coach Marv Levy became emotional when talking about the scene at the stadium on Christmas day.

"About 2:30 p.m., I was getting ready to go home, and I walked outside to see how bad the stadium was," he said. "I looked up in the stands and there were a bunch of people they had just brought in. I guess they were getting $5 an hour to clean the stands out. And I looked up at them and I felt a great sense of admiration for them. Most of them were homeless. . . . I stopped and talked to them for a while. It was on my mind when I left them. And I turned around and said to them, 'I hope my team shows as much spunk tomorrow as you're showing right now.'"

It was the coldest game in team history at that point, and it was a subject of conversation by players, coaches, and fans alike. But since it had playoff implications for both teams, the game still drew a big crowd. If the Jets won, they would reach the postseason. If the Bills won, they would wrap up another division title.

The Bills' offense did its best in the early going, taking the opening kickoff and going 71 yards in 10 plays for the

Thurman Thomas didn't let some cold weather chill the Bills' play.
CREDIT GETTY IMAGES

opening touchdown. Thurman Thomas fumbled somewhere around the goal line, but the officials—who didn't have the benefit of replay at that point in league history—ruled it a score. Later in the first period, New York's Johnny Johnson caught a screen pass from Boomer Esiason and he took off on a 24-yard scoring play that tied it. It was New York's first touchdown pass in six games.

Steve Christie had a couple of field goals in the second quarter to give the Bills a 13–7 lead, but Esiason got that score back on a pass to Chris Burkett. The ex-Bill did a little skating in the back of the end zone after making the catch but held on to the ball. Blanchard's extra point put the Jets up by a point midway through the third quarter.

It looked like the Bills might be in trouble. The team had three turnovers to self-destruct at times. But Christie converted his third field goal in as many tries, this one from 40 yards out with 3:48 left in the fourth quarter, to give Buffalo the 16–14 lead.

There was still time for a rally. New York moved down the field in the final minutes, and lined up for a potential game-winning kick with 53 seconds left. But Blanchard missed from 42 yards out. He said the ball "looked like it was going right down the middle and then it started drifting left."

"When it got about 10 yards from the goal post, a gust of wind just moved it out," Bills running back Kenneth Davis added. "It was that typical Rich Stadium wind."

BOX SCORE

	1ST	2ND	3RD	4TH	FINAL
N.Y. JETS (L, 8-7)	7	0	7	0	14
BUFFALO (W, 11-4)	7	6	0	3	16

SCORING SUMMARY:

QTR	TEAM	PLAY
1ST	BUF.	Thomas 2-yard run (Christie kick)
1ST	NYJ.	Esiason 24-yard pass to Johnson (Blanchard kick)
2ND	BUF.	Christie 38-yard field goal
2ND	BUF.	Christie 36-yard field goal
3RD	NYJ.	Esiason 6-yard pass to Burkett (Blanchard kick)
4TH	BUF.	Christie 40-yard field goal

ATTENDANCE: 70,817

Christie, who had developed a reputation as a clutch kicker in a stadium that every such specialist found difficult to solve, was 3 for 3 on the day in field goals, while Blanchard was 0 for 3. "We practiced Thursday [indoors] and after practice, we came out on the turf, which was frozen, and we realized we had to change a few things," Christie said. "I had to change my alignment. I take a sharp angle to the ball and I couldn't do it. It was too slippery."

The win made it five AFC East championships in six years for Buffalo, and provided more heartache for a Jets franchise that has specialized in it since its 1969 Super Bowl win. "Those guys—their chances went out the window with that kick," Bills linebacker Cornelius Bennett said. "Our chances became a reality."

Ranked No. 46 of 50 by the authors.

NOTEWORTHY: *New York linebacker Kyle Clifton had 17 tackles and an interception. The teams combined for 488 passing yards and 698 total yards. Bills quarterback Jim Kelly finished 20 of 31 for 256 yards. Buffalo linebacker Darryl Talley had his 1,000th career tackle. The Bills had sold out the previous 25 games before this one, but any unsold seats were understandable. "I'm not sure if I was a spectator, I could have stood it out there," Buffalo center Kent Hull said. "My hat's off to them." The Bills led the NFL in attendance for the sixth year in a row, drawing 626,784 for the season, the second highest in team history.*

AFC PLAYOFFS

JANUARY 15, 1994

RAIDERS At BILLS

THIS WASN'T a football game; it was a Johnny Carson joke.

How cold was it?

It was so cold that soft drinks quickly turned into popsicles. It was so cold that media members used credit cards to scrape the windows in the press box in a losing battle to keep them clear of frost. It was so cold that the toes of Bills' linebacker Darryl Talley were still numb well after the end of the game.

It was the coldest game ever played by the Bills, anywhere. It was also one of the coldest games in NFL history. The temperature was zero degrees, a rarity in Western New York during the day. The wind chill at one point reached a ridiculous -32 degrees. No wonder about a quarter of the fans decided to stay home that day and watch it on television, even though the winner of the contest would advance to the AFC Championship Game.

About 130 people were treated for medical issues. Seven of them went to the hospital. "Everyone here is on a mission right now," Glenn Gaviller of Lockport told *The Buffalo News*. "No. 1 is to win. No. 2 is to survive." Cheryl Spaulding of East Amherst and her family all brought thermal sleeping bags, and she had a plan. "You just don't move. You don't get out," she told *The News*.

Yet, somehow, someway, the Bills and Raiders stayed warm enough to put on a good offensive show at Rich Stadium. No one probably saw that coming, particularly after a scoreless first quarter.

The Raiders more or less dominated much of the second quarter. They took a 17–6 lead at one point. But Thurman Thomas scored a late

Wide receiver Bill Brooks scored the game-winning touchdown for Buffalo.
CREDIT ROBERT L. SMITH, ORCHARD PARK, NY

Jim Kelly survived some brutal weather to lead the Bills to a playoff win.
CREDIT ROBERT L. SMITH, ORCHARD PARK, NY

touchdown to move the Bills within four points. Buffalo was still in the game despite having the ball for less than seven minutes in the first half.

"It was very important," Buffalo defense end Bruce Smith said about the late score. "It was probably the most important drive of the game. There's a tremendous difference being down four points as opposed to 11 points. That motivated us to come out in the second half and achieve the things we did."

Buffalo took the lead early in the third quarter on a pass from Jim Kelly to Bill Brooks, and soon added another field goal. However, Jeff Hostetler—you might remember him as the Super Bowl quarterback for the Giants against the Bills in 1991—hit Tim Brown with a bomb to put Los Angeles back in front. The Bills had a quarter to figure out a way to keep their streak of consecutive Super Bowl appearances going instead of ending at three.

Buffalo had one big edge as the minutes ticked down: The Raiders had almost no offense. They didn't have a single drive in the second half that lasted more than three plays. Their only first down came on the long touchdown pass.

"In the second half, we went to an eight-man front," Bills' defensive coordinator Walt Corey said. "Before, we played with a seven-man front. It was one of those things you had to take a shot at it, and it worked."

The second half was one of Kelly's finest hours as a pro quarterback. He threw to Brooks again for what was the game-winning touchdown. The Raiders still had about seven minutes left for a comeback, but Smith's sack of Hostetler ended a possession. From there, Buffalo ran out the clock, as running back Kenneth Davis picked up three first downs.

Kelly was 17 of 25 for 192 yards and two scores in the second half under very difficult conditions.

"Before the game and all during the course of the week, I kept telling the five guys up front that the key to this ballgame was good pass protection," he said. "We thought that these were probably going to be the toughest four guys that we were going to face this year. On both touchdown passes, I needed that extra two seconds to throw the football, and they gave it to me."

"Jim gave a championship performance in a championship-type game," Bills coach Marv Levy said. "He's a tough-minded quarterback. It was his kind of game in his kind of weather with his kind of teammates. He was our catalyst."

Somehow, someway, the Bills had figured out a way to win again. They had earned the right to play one more home game, and with it the chance to return to the Super Bowl again.

"It was a great day to play football," Buffalo center Kent Hull said. Then he added, "Well, maybe it wasn't that great a day."

Ranked No. 31 of 50 by the authors.

BOX SCORE

	1ST	2ND	3RD	4TH	FINAL
L.A. RAIDERS (L)	0	17	6	0	23
BUFFALO (W)	0	13	9	7	29

SCORING SUMMARY:

QTR	TEAM	PLAY
2ND	LAR.	Jaeger 30-yard field goal
2ND	BUF.	Davis 1-yard run (kick missed)
2ND	LAR.	McCallum 1-yard run (Jaeger kick)
2ND	LAR.	McCallum 1-yard run (Jaeger kick)
2ND	BUF.	Thomas 8-yard run (Christie kick)
3RD	BUF.	Kelly 25-yard pass to Brooks (kick blocked)
3RD	BUF.	Christie 29-yard field goal
3RD	LAR.	Hostetler 86-yard pass to Brown (kick missed)
4TH	BUF.	Kelly 22-yard pass to Brooks (Christie kick)

ATTENDANCE: 61,923

NOTEWORTHY: *Kelly finished 27 of 37 for 287 yards. Steve Tasker had a 67-yard kickoff return, the longest in Bills' playoff history at that point. Elbert Dubenion had the old record at 62 yards in 1963. Hostetler's 86-yard pass to Brown set a Buffalo playoff record for longest play against the Bills. It was the smallest crowd for a Bills home game, non-strike, since 56,534 turned out for a game with Houston on September 20, 1987.*

Thurman Thomas was never better than he was in this game.
CREDIT GETTY IMAGES

JANUARY 23, 1994

CHIEFS At BILLS

THERE WERE TWO big stories surrounding this AFC Championship Game—one for each team.

The Bills were trying to reach the Super Bowl for the fourth straight time. The Miami Dolphins had done it three times in a row (1971 to 1973), a stretch that included a perfect 17–0 record in the 1972 season. The Bills had equaled that number in the early 1990s with three straight appearances—all losses. Great teams don't last forever, but the Bills already had shown their resilience by putting themselves in a position to return again.

"Like it or not, we're here," quarterback Jim Kelly said. "There's no pressure on us. We're the team that nobody wanted here. We're the team nobody thought would be here."

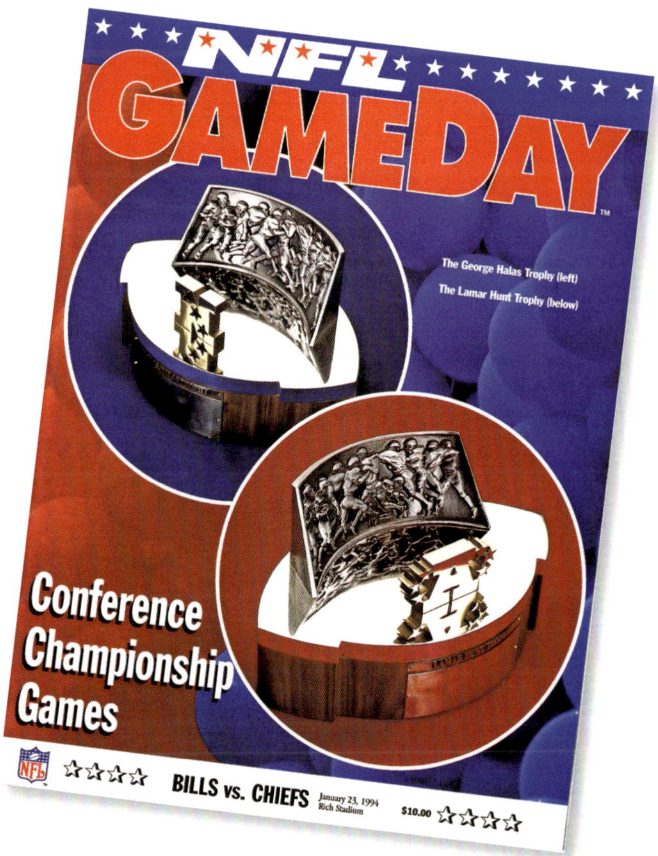

"The whole team feels the same way. We want to get there [another Super Bowl]," Buffalo linebacker Cornelius Bennett said. "'In your face' to everyone who didn't believe in us."

The more sentimental story involved the Kansas City Chiefs. Their quarterback was ready for a familiar task in an unfamiliar uniform. Joe Montana was put in charge of getting the Chiefs to the Super Bowl for the first time since their win in January 1970.

Montana already had guaranteed himself a ticket to first-ballot admission to the Pro Football Hall of Fame with an incredible run of success in his first decade as a pro with the San Francisco 49ers. Montana won four Super Bowls in that time, and he was considered a strong candidate to be ranked as the best quarterback ever. But in 1993, the 49ers made room for Steve Young to become a starter when they traded Montana to Kansas City. It was a good fit. Kansas City went 11–5 to win the AFC West, and beat Pittsburgh and Houston to advance to the AFC's title game.

"His name and reputation speak for itself," Bills defensive end Bruce Smith said. "He's not just a great quarterback, he's a phenomenal one, probably the best whoever played this game. And he's just that great a leader."

One question loomed over the 1994 contest: Does Joe still have his old magic?

We found out relatively quickly that Montana wasn't going to be the key figure in the game. Neither was Kelly, speaking of future Hall of Fame quarterbacks. That distinction would belong to another football legend, Buffalo running back Thurman Thomas.

The Bills wasted little time in scoring first. Thomas finished off the drive by breaking through a crowded line to find clear sailing to the end zone. Kansas City responded as Nick Lowery kicked two field goals to narrow Buffalo's lead to 7–6. Thomas went back to work, boosting a drive with a 32-yard run and then almost walking in to the end zone for a touchdown.

He had 96 yards rushing in the second period alone. "He had a glaze over his eyes," guard John Davis said. "It's hard to explain but he went out there and did everything we asked him."

When Steve Christie added two field goals for the Bills before the half, it put the score at 20–6—comfortable but not safe. The Chiefs got one of those scores back, as Marcus Allen plunged the ball into the end zone. But shortly before that, Montana suffered a concussion and was out for the rest of the game.

That meant Dave Krieg had to do the heavy lifting for Kansas City. He was all right—16 of 29 for 198 yards—but he also threw an interception and was sacked twice. In other words, Krieg was no Joe Montana—that is, the vintage Joe Montana.

In the fourth quarter, Christie put the Bills up by more than a possession with a short field goal. Fittingly, Thomas soon provided the exclamation point. He ran it in from 3 yards away, and the Bills could pack for the Super Bowl again. Thomas wouldn't be needed to fly the plane to Atlanta, but he'd done everything else to guarantee that Buffalo would go there. The veteran ran the ball 33 times for 186 yards and three scores. For good measure, Thomas caught two passes for 33 yards. He called it "the best day of my six-year career," and there were no arguments.

"I was really pumped up today, because I want to go back to the Super Bowl as much as anybody else on this football team," the running back continued.

He contributed mightily to a couple of other important statistics. Buffalo finished with 30 first downs, and as a team had a franchise-record 229 yards rushing. Kelly had an easy day, completing 17 of 27 passes for 160 yards without a touchdown or interception.

For a franchise that had been on the outside looking in when it came to the title game from 1967 to 1990, four straight appearances were almost beyond belief.

"This is the toughest-minded football team that's ever played the game, in my opinion," coach Marv Levy said. "They are tough-minded, and they've shown it over and over. We fought our way back in."

Ranked No. 22 of 50 by the authors.

BOX SCORE

	1ST	2ND	3RD	4TH	FINAL
KANSAS CITY (L)	6	0	7	0	13
BUFFALO (W)	7	13	0	10	30

SCORING SUMMARY:

QTR	TEAM	PLAY
1ST	BUF.	Thomas 12-yard run (Christie kick)
1ST	K.C.	Lowery 31-yard field goal
1ST	K.C.	Lowery 31-yard field goal
2ND	BUF.	Thomas 3-yard run (Christie kick)
2ND	BUF.	Christie 23-yard field goal
2ND	BUF.	Christie 25-yard field goal
3RD	K.C.	Allen 1-yard run (Lowery kick)
4TH	BUF.	Christie 18-yard field goal
4TH	BUF.	Thomas 3-yard run (Christie kick)

ATTENDANCE: 76,642

NOTEWORTHY: *Montana finished the day 9 of 23 for 125 yards; his passer rating was 39.2. The Bills defense finished the game with two interceptions and four sacks. Buffalo improved its all-time home playoff record in Rich Stadium to 8–0.*

DECEMBER 30, 1995

DOLPHINS At BILLS

IN 1995, Don Shula hadn't been patrolling the sidelines for the Miami Dolphins forever. It only seemed that way.

Shula's first head coaching job came when the Baltimore Colts hired him in 1963. He stayed until after the 1969 season, when he jumped to the Dolphins. Shula arrived in Miami just in time for the NFL's realignment in 1970. Fatefully, the Bills and Dolphins were put in the same division, which meant Shula and company would visit Buffalo at least once every year.

In 1995, the 65-year-old Shula was rumored to be having problems in his relationship with Dolphins owner Wayne Huizenga. Shula already owned the NFL record for lifetime coaching victories, and he didn't have many worlds left to conquer. At the end of the regular season, Huizenga said about Shula's status, "Don's got another year if he wants it."

Miami squeezed into the playoffs that season with a 9–7 record, and that meant a trip to Buffalo to play the Bills—the AFC East champions at 10–6. Little did Shula know that his last trip to Rich Stadium would be a good-sized nightmare. Entering the postseason, Shula probably was aware that Bills' head coach Marv Levy had a 16–5 record in games against Shula. (Buffalo had been 3–30 against Shula until Levy's arrival.)

"Marv and his staff deserve as much credit for the success that we've had against the Dolphins as anybody," Steve Tasker of the Bills said.

The Bills moved right down the field on their first possession, and Thurman Thomas took it in for the opening touchdown. Miami received the next kickoff and went nowhere again. Thomas's 26 yards rushing on the next drive moved the ball close enough for Steve Christie to kick a field goal. The Bills had a 10–0 lead, and the Dolphins hadn't even picked up a first down.

Early in the second quarter, Thomas' 32-yard run set up a nice scoring sprint by Darick Holmes. Only minutes later, Kelly completed a pass to Tasker for a score. It was 24–0 for Buffalo, and the Dolphins had done little. Miami supplied a fitting outcome for the half when Pete Stoyanovich missed a 53-yard field goal.

No lead against quarterback Dan Marino and the Dolphins was safe, but this felt close to secure as the third quarter wound down. Christie kicked another field goal after a good-sized drive stalled on the Miami 5-yard line.

Shula and the Dolphins had given up running the ball at that point; they needed points in a hurry. Marino put a few completions together, and one was a touchdown to O.J. McDuffie near the start of the fourth quarter. The Bills soon responded in an unusual way: Tim Tindale rumbled 44 yards for a score. It was the only touchdown of Tindale's relatively short career of 37 total games.

The scoring went back and forth from there. Marino hit Randal Hill on a bomb for a score, Christie kicked another field goal, and Miami's Terry Kirby scored on a short run. But it was all irrelevant in a sense. Buffalo went on to claim a 37–22 win over Miami.

The story of the game was the way the Bills ran the ball. They piled up 341 yards on the ground, the

Tim Tindale runs for his only career touchdown in the NFL.
CREDIT ROBERT L. SMITH, ORCHARD PARK, NY

BOX SCORE

	1ST	2ND	3RD	4TH	FINAL
MIAMI (L)	0	0	0	22	22
BUFFALO (W)	10	14	3	10	37

SCORING SUMMARY:

QTR	TEAM	PLAY
1ST	BUF.	Thomas 1-yard run (Christie kick)
1ST	BUF.	Christie 48-yard field goal
2ND	BUF.	Holmes 21-yard run (Christie kick)
2ND	BUF.	Kelly 37-yard pass to Tasker (Christie kick)
3RD	BUF.	Christie 23-yard field goal
4TH	MIA.	Marino 5-yard pass to McDuffie (Stoyanovich kick)
4TH	BUF.	Tindale 44-yard run (Christie kick)
4TH	MIA.	Marino 45-yard pass to Hill (Stoyanovich kick)
4TH	BUF.	Christie 42-yard field goal
4TH	MIA.	Kirby 1-yard run (Marino pass to McDuffie)

ATTENDANCE: 73,103

second-biggest total in the NFL's postseason history, on 52 carries. Thomas led the way with 158 yards.

"The offensive line did a great job of blocking and it enabled me to pick whatever hole I wanted to go through," Thomas said. "We were very surprised that they stayed in the same defense that they played two weeks ago here when we clinched the AFC East."

"I've never been part of something like that since college, running the wishbone, and that was a long time ago," Bills center Kent Hull said. "If you can run the football, offensively you can do anything."

Marino finished the day with an arm that must have needed an offseason to recover from the effort. He was 33 of 64 for 422 yards, two touchdowns and three interceptions.

"I'm kind of in shock," Marino said. "I don't know what else to say; I've never been beaten like this. We weren't even in the game. For them to dominate us in every facet like this, it's tough."

Less than a week later, Shula was no longer the coach of the Dolphins. He announced his retirement from football. The playoff game in Buffalo was his last. Shula was 2–9 in his last 11 visits to Rich Stadium.

"This week has been soul-searching . . . gut-wrenching," Shula said at a news conference announcing his retirement. "I'd be lying if I didn't say I'm going to feel out of place when I'm not down on the field this fall for the first time in 43 years."

Ranked No. 42 of 50 by the authors.

NOTEWORTHY: *The win was the Bills' ninth straight in home playoff games, extending their NFL record. The teams combined for 1,038 total yards, breaking the NFL postseason record. Kelly was happy to hand the ball off so much, but he did go 12 of 22 for 195 yards.*

DECEMBER 28, 1996

JAGUARS At BILLS

THE BILLS were in the midst of one of the greatest eras in their history. In the nine years between 1988 and 1996, the team qualified for the playoffs eight times, only missing out in 1994. The run included four consecutive trips to the Super Bowl, an unprecedented event in league history. It topped the period in the 1960s for sustained dominance when Buffalo won back-to-back AFL titles. The Super Bowl appearances probably give that group an edge on the current Bills, which had its sixth straight postseason appearance (and seventh in eight years) in the 2024 season.

The 1996 Bills had fallen off a bit by this time, even if it was hard to admit that the core group of players was starting to get old together. The hope was that there was still enough life in the Old Gang for one last playoff push together. The team went 10–6 in the regular season—good enough to claim a wild-card playoff spot. Their regular season earned the Bills the chance to play that postseason opener at home against Jacksonville.

The Jaguars were the upstarts at the playoff party. The team only started play in the NFL the year before in 1995, and finished 4–12. Everyone was surprised that Jacksonville improved to 9–7 a season later, which included five straight wins to sneak into the postseason.

This was a dangerous team, but the Bills had far more experience and the home-field advantage—which was valuable since the team went 7–1 in Rich Stadium that year and was 67–14 overall there under head coach Marv Levy. The Bills had won all nine of their playoff home games in that building. Jim Kelly had finished his worst regular season as a pro—14 touchdowns and 19 interceptions—but surely he had something left in that magical right arm.

It didn't take long for this game to show that it was going to be a thrill ride of a matchup. Kelly threw a short pass to Thurman Thomas for the opening score of the day. But soon after that Kelly tried an awkward shovel pass that looked like an error

Jim Kelly is helped off the field in his last moments as a Bills' player.
CREDIT ROBERT L. SMITH, ORCHARD PARK, NY

12
76

in judgment immediately. Those feelings grew as Clyde Simmons caught the pass and took it into the end zone for the Jaguars. It was Kelly's fifth "pick-six" pass of the season. Thomas added another touchdown on a short run, only to see Jacksonville score the next 10 points. At least Steve Christie kicked a tying field goal late in the second quarter to tie the contest.

The teams traded field goals in the third quarter, so the last 15 minutes of play (or more) would decide the outcome. When Jeff Burris of the Bills returned an interception for a touchdown, the Bills had a 27–20 lead . . . and it looked as if the Old Gang had figured out a way to win once again.

The Upstarts, though, weren't convinced. Jacksonville moved 65 yards down the field, and Brunell's screen pass to Jimmy Smith tied the game. The news for the Bills turned worse from there. Kelly was clobbered by Jacksonville's Chris Hudson and fumbled the ball away with 7:13 left. Kelly looked as if he didn't know where he was because of a possible head injury. When he was carted off to the locker room, done for the day, a sense of foreboding came over the Bills and their supporters.

From there, even luck was in the Jaguars' corner. Mike Hollis had a 45-yard field goal attempt that hit the upright and fell through the goal posts. "Nothing happened," Hollis said about the near-miss. "It was a great kick. The wind was what happened."

BOX SCORE

	1ST	2ND	3RD	4TH	FINAL
JACKSONVILLE (W)	10	7	3	10	30
BUFFALO (L)	14	3	3	7	27

SCORING SUMMARY:

QTR	TEAM	PLAY
1ST	BUF.	Kelly 7-yard pass to Thomas (Christie kick)
1ST	JAX.	Simmons 20-yard interception return (Hollis kick)
1ST	BUF.	Thomas 2-yard run (Christie kick)
1ST	JAX.	Hollis 27-yard field goal
2ND	JAX.	Means 30-yard run (Hollis kick)
2ND	BUF.	Christie 33-yard field goal
3RD	BUF.	Christie 47-yard field goal
3RD	JAX.	Hollis 24-yard field goal
4TH	BUF.	Burris 38-yard interception return (Christie kick)
4TH	JAX.	Brunell 2-yard pass to Smith (Holliskick)
4TH	JAX.	Hollis 45-yard field goal

ATTENDANCE: 70,213

There was still time for a last gasp from the Bills, but backup quarterback Todd Collins couldn't move the team on one possession and fumbled the ball away on the second. The Jaguars were 30–27 winners. The Bills' season was over.

As it turned out, this game would be the last time this magical group that had accomplished so much over the years would be together in its entirety. Kelly's cart ride was the last time we'd see him in a Bills uniform. He announced his retirement early in the offseason. That opening touchdown pass to Thomas would be the last he'd throw in his brilliant career, and the fumble was his last play. While the Bills still had a good nucleus, the team would take on a different personality in the immediate future without Kelly.

In other words, the era wasn't over yet, but you could see it in the distance.

Ranked No. 34 of 50 by the authors.

NOTEWORTHY: *Thomas set an NFL record by scoring a touchdown in his eighth straight playoff game. The Jaguars had a big edge in rushing yardage, 184 to 92. Natrone Means ran over several Buffalo defenders on his way to 175 yards. That set a record for most rushing yards allowed by the Bills in a playoff game. The Bills had a total of four fumbles, losing two of them, and had an interception to finish with three turnovers. The temperature at kickoff was 49 degrees, making it the warmest playoff game ever staged in Buffalo.*

SEPTEMBER 21, 1997

COLTS At BILLS

TODD COLLINS had replaced Jim Kelly as the Bills' new starting quarterback with the future Hall of Famer's retirement at the end of the 1996 season. This game was Collins' fourth start of 1997 and his eighth career start. His performances had been up-and-down at best.

Meanwhile, Indianapolis, under head coach Lindy Infante with quarterback Jim Harbaugh, running back Marshall Faulk and receiver Marvin Harrison, had been a playoff team in 1996 and were expected to compete for the AFC South Division title in 1997. However, the Colts had started 0–3 and were yet to score an offensive touchdown. Put all that together, and this matchup figured to be unpredictable . . . and it more than lived up to that description.

The Bills decided to help Indianapolis right from the start of the game. Following a stalled Colts' drive, Mitchell Galloway muffed a punt and the Colts recovered at the Bills' 20-yard line. Three plays later, the Colts were in the end zone. Later in the first quarter, Indianapolis took advantage of another short field and Faulk scored on a 10-yard run to put the Colts up 14–0.

Following Indy's second-quarter field goal, the game became a comedy of errors for the Bills and a field goal fest for the Colts. Collins threw an interception; Blanchard kicked a field goal. Collins fumbled; Blanchard kicked a field goal; Collins fumbled again; Blanchard kicked another field goal. Suddenly it was 26–0 and it should have been a lot more.

At that point in the game the Bills had six total yards of offense, one first down, and four turnovers. Bills coach Marv Levy said, "Everything went wrong. We were uptight and not playing with confidence. It was follies out there."

To Collins's credit and with a little help from a veteran teammate, he stuck with it. "I went over and told him, 'Jim has been in this situation before, where he's had a bad start, where he's thrown three interceptions, but he always hung in there," Thurman Thomas recalled. "I told Todd, 'I have faith in you.'"

The young quarterback answered his poor play with two scoring drives before halftime, highlighted by his 16-yard touchdown pass to Lonnie Johnson. "Guys did a great job hanging in there, and fighting together and knowing that we could still come back," receiver Quinn Early said. "It was 26–10 at the half, and we felt we could move the football."

Buffalo further cut into the Colts' lead in the third quarter on Antowain Smith's 15-yard touchdown run but failed on a two-point conversion attempt. The two teams went into the fourth quarter with Indianapolis still holding a two-score lead, 26–16.

Blanchard converted his fifth field goal early in the final period, set up by another Buffalo muffed punt. "It could have gotten really ugly, but the defense kept their poise and held them to a field goal and that's our goal, not to let them score a touchdown after a turnover," nose tackle Ted Washington said.

The Bills then, somewhat unexpectedly, went on a scoring rampage. During the next nine minutes the Bills ran 15 plays, picked up 167 yards and scored three touchdowns to take a 37–29 lead. Smith's 54-yard breakaway run capped the scoring for Buffalo. But the Colts were not done. Reserve quarterback Paul Justin replaced Harbaugh after the future NFL coach took a nasty late hit, and Justin drove Indianapolis for a touchdown in less than a minute. Bills safety Kurt Schulz broke up a pass to Harrison to deny the Colts a two-point conversion that would have tied the game.

Though only 14 seconds remained, the game was still not over. Indianapolis recovered its onside kick. Justin threw two Hail Mary passes to the end zone but the second one was picked off by Ken Irvin, enabling the Bills to prevail.

"Coming back from 26 points down was a little scary." Collins said, "I knew we were capable of coming back. I'd like to get on these guys early, so it doesn't come down to the wire every time." Cornerback Thomas Smith added, "That was crazy, one of the craziest games I've ever seen. It was wild, but that resiliency that we have known in the past came through."

Ranked No. 28 of 50 by the authors.

BOX SCORE

	1ST	2ND	3RD	4TH	FINAL
INDIANAPOLIS (L, 0-4)	14	12	0	9	35
BUFFALO (W, 2-2)	0	10	6	21	37

SCORING SUMMARY:

QTR	TEAM	PLAY
1ST	IND.	Harbaugh 10-yard pass to Bailey (Blanchard kick)
1ST	IND.	Faulk 10-yard run (Blanchard kick)
2ND	IND.	Blanchard 39-yard field goal
2ND	IND.	Blanchard 36-yard field goal
2ND	IND.	Blanchard 49-yard field goal
2ND	IND.	Blanchard 22-yard field goal
2ND	BUF.	Collins 16-yard pass to Johnson (Christie kick)
2ND	BUF.	Christie 27-yard field goal
3RD	BUF.	Smith 15-yard run (run failed)
4TH	IND.	Blanchard 25-yard field goal
4TH	BUF.	Collins 4-yard pass to Early (Christie kick)
4TH	BUF.	Smith 1-yard run (Christie kick)
4TH	BUF.	Smith 54-yard run (Christie kick)
4TH	IND.	Justin 2-yard pass to Harrison (pass failed)

ATTENDANCE: 55,340

NOTEWORTHY: *The 26-point deficit the Bills overcame is still the greatest regular season comeback in team history. The Bills' previous greatest comeback in the regular season was 21 points, in a 34–31 win over Miami on October 25, 1987. It was also the third greatest comeback in NFL history to that time. Collins completed 23 of 38 passes for 275 yards. Antowain Smith rushed 12 times for 129 yards and three touchdowns. Smith was named AFC Offensive Player of the Week. Thomas ran for 22 yards and caught five passes for 44. Those yards allowed him to pass Jim Brown for sixth place on the all-time yards from scrimmage list with 14,865 yards.*

Todd Collins was the unlikely hero in Buffalo's huge comeback win.
CREDIT ROBERT L. SMITH, ORCHARD PARK, NY

OCTOBER 18, 1998

JAGUARS At BILLS

DURING THE offseason, the Bills addressed their quarterback position after they decided that Todd Collins was not the team's quarterback of the future. Buffalo signed CFL superstar Doug Flutie. When Ralph Wilson met Flutie for the first time after he signed the contract, the Bills' owner said to him, "So you're our new savior." Then a short time later Buffalo acquired former USC quarterback Rob Johnson from the Jacksonville Jaguars in a trade. At first, a competition was expected

Doug Flutie's heroics might have saved the Bills' franchise for Buffalo.
CREDIT ROBERT L. SMITH, ORCHARD PARK, NY

between the two for the first string spot. However, the Bills signed Johnson to an unprecedented $25 million contract, and he was deemed the starter.

After losing three out of their first four games to start the season, Johnson was knocked out of a game with Indianapolis with torn rib cartilage. Flutie relieved him and led the Bills to a come-from-behind 31–24 victory. Johnson was expected to be out of the lineup for a few weeks.

Meanwhile, the Bills' franchise as a whole had bigger issues lurking in the background. The team had signed a new 15-year lease for the stadium, but the deal had a critical contingency clause. The Bills had to sell $11 million of suites and club seats by December 1 to lock in the agreement for at least five years. Otherwise, Wilson had the option to move the team out of Buffalo. At this point in the season, the Bills were lagging far behind of the sales goal, and the team's fans were getting more anxious by the day. Buffalo really needed to start winning some games and to create some excitement, or the goal seemed unachievable.

Flutie was starting his first game as the quarterback of the Bills against Jacksonville and making his first NFL start in nine years, but his performance against the Colts gave him confidence entering the matchup.

The Jaguars took control of the game at the start. Quarterback Mark Brunell moved his team 69 yards in 16 plays on a drive that was capped off by a one-yard run from Avian Banks. It didn't take Flutie long to respond. Early in the second quarter, he threw a touchdown pass to Eric Moulds to tie the game. Jacksonville added a field goal prior to halftime and went to the break leading the Bills 10–7.

The Jaguars added two more field goals from Mike Hollis in the third quarter sandwiched around Steve Christie's field goal for Buffalo. With Jacksonville in the lead 16–10, the defenses were controlling the game as the clock was winding down. "Everyone on this defense knew we could get the job done," Bills' linebacker John Holecek said. "We held them down when we had to." But it would all be for naught if Flutie could not engineer a game-winning drive.

Buffalo got one more chance with 1:50 left on the clock. Flutie moved Buffalo to the Jaguars' 39-yard line with only 39 seconds left and the Bills without any timeouts. "We were throwing a lot of short stuff," Flutie said. "It was difficult to keep taking nickel and dime. We needed a big play somewhere, the way it was going."

And it was about to come. "I forced myself to keep looking, keep looking down the center of the field," Flutie said. "I never turned my head, but I sneaked a peek to the left [where Moulds was running his route down the sideline]. I saw the safety break to the center of the field [expecting Flutie's pass to go there]. As I let the ball go toward Eric I was still looking into the middle of the field."

Moulds caught Flutie's pass and dove to the end zone. The ball was placed at the 1-yard line with 28 seconds left. Three incomplete passes later, the Bills eventually faced a fourth down and goal.

The play call was an option in which Flutie is supposed either to give the ball to Thurman Thomas or pass it to him. The crowd noise was deafening, and Thomas did not hear the correct play call. When Flutie took the center snap and turned to give the ball to Thomas, the running back had gone the other way. Flutie quickly ad-libbed and bootlegged the ball around the left end, outrunning the defenders into the end zone for one of the most improbable touchdowns in Bills history.

"I called one play, and Thurman thought I called another," Flutie said. "I turned and he wasn't there, so I just took off. . . . It was more fun because I took it in." Christie converted the extra point and Buffalo had a heart-stopping 17–16 victory.

BOX SCORE

	1ST	2ND	3RD	4TH	FINAL
JACKSONVILLE (L, 5-1)	7	3	6	0	16
BUFFALO (W, 3-3)	0	7	3	7	17

SCORING SUMMARY:

QTR	TEAM	PLAY
1ST	JAX.	Banks 1-yard run (Hollis kick)
2ND	BUF.	Flutie 12-yard pass to Moulds (Christie kick)
2ND	JAX.	Hollis 35-yard field goal
3RD	JAX.	Hollis 23-yard field goal
3RD	BUF.	Christie 24-yard field goal
3RD	JAX.	Hollis 27-yard field goal
4TH	BUF.	Flutie 1-yard run (Christie kick)

ATTENDANCE: 77,635

"He's a big-time player who made big-time plays," Bills defensive end Bruce Smith said about Flutie. "His heart's a lot bigger than his size."

Flutie-mania had begun and would engulf the fans of the Bills over the next several weeks as the team made a drive for the playoffs. Even better, the effects of that win on the team's future would be felt for literally decades, as the team reached its revenue goal and stayed put.

Ranked No. 5 of 50 by the authors.

NOTEWORTHY: *The Bills' offense produced 337 yards of total offense. Flutie threw for 228 yards and one touchdown. Buffalo's defense held Brunell to only 119 yards passing and sacked him three times. The Bills reported they sold all the Doug Flutie jerseys they had inside the stadium—before the game.*

SEPTEMBER 7, 2003

PATRIOTS At BILLS

BILLS FANS certainly remember how the Miami Dolphins beat their favorite team 20 straight times during the 1970s to set an NFL record for domination by one team over another. Surely, they thought, such a losing streak could never happen again to the Bills. Yet, it almost did.

The Bills had defeated the New England Patriots on November 5, 2000, at home in overtime, but lost the rematch in Foxboro a few weeks later. The Patriots also won the next four meetings between the teams (with Tom Brady starting at quarterback in all of them), and won a Super Bowl along the way. The schedule-maker seemed anxious to see if Buffalo could avoid a sixth straight loss to New England, as the Bills and Patriots opened the 2003 season at Ralph Wilson Stadium.

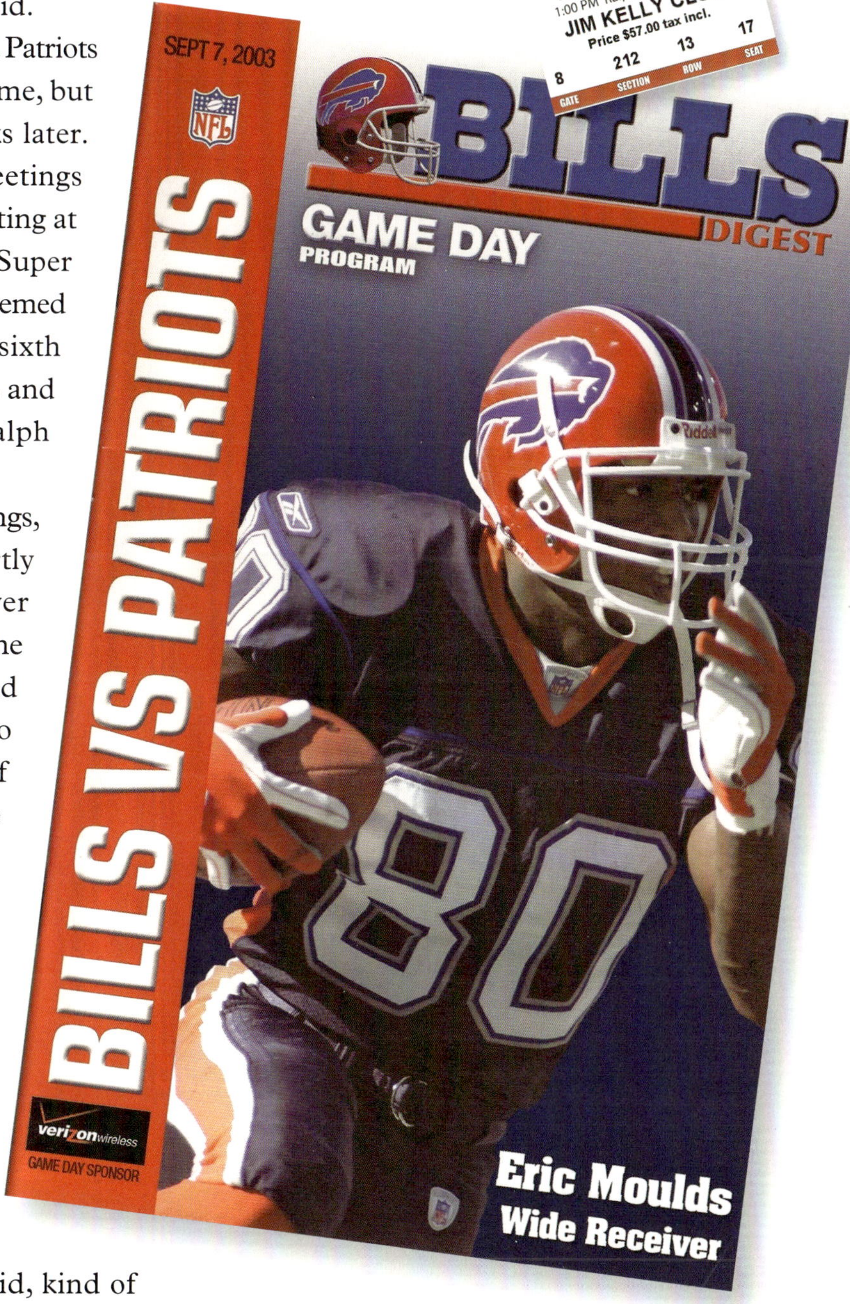

Just to add a little drama to the proceedings, a player personnel move took place shortly before the game. Defensive back Lawyer Milloy had refused to take a pay cut from the Patriots in the offseason. So New England cut the veteran, who had played in the Pro Bowl the previous season and was one of the team's captains, on September 2. The Bills needed about 24 hours to sign Milloy to a five-year contract—four days before the season opener.

Imagine the feeling that Milloy had when he ran out on the field for the player introductions before the start of the game. It was quite a change for someone who had been always booed upon arrival in Orchard Park in the past.

"It was a welcoming feeling," Milloy said. "From leaving Boston the way I did, kind of rejected, to be coming here and getting my name called out and getting the fans going, it just felt like I had been here my whole career. It was great. It was football."

The Bills set the tone right away, moving 80 yards as Travis Henry scored on a short plunge. From there, Buffalo doubled its lead as ex-Patriots quarterback Drew Bledsoe threw to Dave Moore.

About three minutes later, the defense made the play that everyone remembers from that game. Brady tried to throw a screen pass, but it was intercepted by defensive lineman Sam Adams. Adams, who weighed in at about 340 pounds before lunch, rumbled 37 untouched yards for the touchdown. It was quite a way to celebrate his first game with the team.

"Until he intercepted that pass, I thought I could outrun him," joked 85-year-old team owner Ralph Wilson. "I didn't know he could run that fast. When the ball is thrown and a 370-pound defensive tackle picks it out of the air and runs it into the end zone, things were going our way."

Amazingly, Adams told a teammate before the game that he planned to return an interception for a touchdown. "I kind of looked at him like 'Yeah, right,'" wide receiver Eric Moulds said.

If it had been anyone but the Patriots, the Bills and their fans might have felt confident of a victory at halftime after taking a 21–0 lead. Even so, the Buffalo defense continued its strong performance in the second half. Buffalo finished the game with four interceptions and two sacks, limiting Brady to 123 yards passing in the process.

"Our defense—jeez, they were tremendous out there," Bledsoe said.

Milloy was part of the solution for the Bills, as he took part in every play but one during the

Sam Adams is off to the races for an unexpected touchdown.
CREDIT GETTY IMAGES

first three quarters. The defensive back deflected one pass that turned into an interception by Nate Clements, and he had a sack as well.

"What I realized today, which I didn't have a chance to realize in the one practice I had here and all the studying I had, is that I'm on a good team," Milloy said.

Henry duplicated his touchdown in the fourth quarter, and Lindell added a field goal to finish

BOX SCORE

	1ST	2ND	3RD	4TH	FINAL
NEW ENGLAND (L, 0-1)	0	0	0	0	0
BUFFALO (W, 1-0)	7	14	0	10	31

SCORING SUMMARY:

QTR	TEAM	PLAY
1ST	BUF.	Henry 1-yard run (Lindell kick)
2ND	BUF.	Bledsoe 7-yard pass to Moore (Lindell kick)
2ND	BUF.	Adams 37-yard interception return (Lindell kick)
4TH	BUF.	Henry 9-yard run (Lindell kick)
4TH	BUF.	Lindell 44-yard field goal

ATTENDANCE: 73,262

the scoring. The result was a shocking 31–0 victory. These Bills weren't going to lose 20 in a row to the Patriots.

"They outplayed us in every phase of the game," Patriots coach Bill Belichick said. "They beat us every way they could. We just didn't play well, coach well, or do anything well. They deserved to beat us. And they deserved to beat us by the score they did."

The rematch went a little differently. In the last game of the regular season, the Bills fell behind 28–0 by halftime and lost by a familiar score of 31–0. Brady finished with four touchdown passes. That Patriots' win in December 2003 was followed by 15 more consecutive victories against Buffalo. In other words, New England won 20 of 21 games over the Bills. The exception was the memorable Opening Day of 2003.

At least it wasn't 20 of 20.

Ranked No. 21 of 50 by the authors.

NOTEWORTHY: *Henry ran the ball 28 times for 86 yards. In one 22-play span in the second half, the running back touched the ball 17 times. This was Buffalo's most one-sided Opening Day win since 1992, a 40–7 win over the Rams, and the Bills' first shutout since 1999 of Philadelphia. Bills legend Joe DeLamielleure was honored at halftime, as he received his Pro Football Hall of Fame ring. The so-called "Electric Company"—the linemen from the 1973 Bills' team—were celebrating the 30th anniversary of O.J. Simpson's 2,003-yard season.*

JANUARY 2, 2005

STEELERS At BILLS

IT WAS AS IF an entire region was preparing for a party.

The Bills hadn't qualified for the NFL playoffs since the 1999 season. That was five years before the Steelers arrived in town to close out the 2004 campaign (although the game was played in 2005). Buffalo had a chance to end that drought with a victory in the season finale. Even more impressively, the Bills had a chance to be the first team since 1992 (and second team ever) to reach the postseason after starting 0–4. (They did need a little help in the form of a Jets' or Broncos' loss, but they had no control over that.)

Buffalo had won six straight games to move into this position. A seventh victory might make it all worthwhile. "Every week has been pressure, so we know how to deal with it," receiver Eric Moulds said. "We'll just go out and play and see what happens."

Yes, the Steelers came into the game with a 14–1 record. But Pittsburgh had absolutely nothing at stake, so there was no reason to give its best players anything but a rest. Have a seat on the bench, Ben Roethlisberger, and rest those bruised ribs. Don't get off the bus, Jerome Bettis, and stay off that sprained ankle. The Bills couldn't have asked for a better situation under the circumstances.

It didn't take long to figure out that beating the Steelers wasn't going to be easy even against some second-stringers. Pittsburgh punted on its first possession, only to have Buffalo's Nate Clements fumble it away to Larry Foote of the Steelers. The visitors soon capitalized with a short field goal. The Bills answered as Willis McGahee scored the go-ahead touchdown. Yet the Steelers responded with a nice drive of their own for a score. It was going to be one of those days.

Foote's interception of Drew Bledsoe's pass put Pittsburgh in business deep in Buffalo territory, and Jeff Reed kicked another field goal to make it 13–7, Steelers. Reed struck again later in the period, but that was negated by Rian Lindell's 37-yard in the final seconds of the half.

Drew Bledsoe couldn't prevent the Bills from suffering a crushing loss.
CREDIT GETTY IMAGES

The Bills had the only score of the third period, as Clements intercepted Tommy Maddox's pass and ran 30 yards for a touchdown. It was the only score of the quarter, and Buffalo had a 17–16 lead with a little more than 15 minutes to go. More importantly, Steelers' regulars were starting to become difficult to find on the field, as they were given the rest of the day off.

Enter Willie Parker, who had done little in the game until that point. Parker promptly went 58 yards to set up another field goal by Reed, and the Bills had lost the lead. "It certainly changed the flow of the game," Bills coach Mike Mularkey said. "You can't allow that to happen."

On the third play of the next possession, Bledsoe was sacked and fumbled. James Harrison of the Steelers ran it into the end zone for an absolutely huge touchdown. Pittsburgh had needed less than two minutes in the fourth quarter to take a 26–17 lead.

Then came the sequence that people remember. The Steelers wanted to run off time, so they kept giving the ball to Parker. He kept chewing up yardage and seconds. Pittsburgh came up with a 15-play drive that took about nine minutes off the clock. Parker ran the ball on 12 of those plays. The Steelers added a field goal to lead 29–17 with 2:27 left, and it was time to cancel the party.

Buffalo did stage a hurry-up drive against Pittsburgh's prevent defense, and McGahee scored a touchdown to cut the margin. But when Ike Taylor of the Steelers grabbed an onside kick attempt, it was time for the Bills to schedule Locker Cleanout Day. Their season was over.

"Their backups are National Football League players," Mularkey said. "This is not the NCAA and you're going to get guys who can't play. They all can play."

Parker finished with 102 yards, almost all of them in the last 16 minutes. He became one of the major villains associated with the Bills' playoff drought of that era.

"It's a blessing to get in there and show my talents off," Parker said of his performance. "It was just a matter of getting out there and making plays."

The shock of the outcome was mixed with disappointment after the game. The Jets did indeed lose to the Rams (in overtime). Buffalo wouldn't come this close to the playoffs for, amazingly, more than a decade.

"It hurts bad, real bad," defensive tackle Pat Williams said. "I can't even say right now. There's no words for it."

Ranked No. 43 of 50 by the authors.

BOX SCORE

	1ST	2ND	3RD	4TH	FINAL
PITTSBURGH (W, 15-1)	10	6	0	13	29
BUFFALO (L, 9-7)	7	3	7	7	24

SCORING SUMMARY:

QTR	TEAM	PLAY
1ST	PIT.	Reed 22-yard field goal
1ST	BUF.	McGahee 3-yard run (Lindell kick)
1ST	PIT.	Maddox 16-yard pass to Randle El (Reed kick)
2ND	PIT.	Reed 21-yard field goal
2ND	PIT.	Reed 31-yard field goal
2ND	BUF.	Lindell 37-yard field goal
3RD	BUF.	Clements 30-yard interception return (Lindell kick)
4TH	PIT.	Reed 37-yard field goal
4TH	PIT.	Harrison 18-yard fumble return (Reed kick)
4TH	PIT.	Reed 33-yard field goal
4TH	BUF.	McGahee 1-yard run

ATTENDANCE: 73,414

NOTEWORTHY: *Maddox finished 12 of 24 for only 120 yards and two interceptions, while Bledsoe only threw for 189 yards. The Steelers had more than a 10-minute advantage in time of possession. Lindell finished the season converting 24 of 28 field-goal attempts, tying him for the second-best percentage in team history.*

OCTOBER 8, 2007

COWBOYS At BILLS

IN THE 2007 SEASON, the Bills were almost in the middle of their seemingly endless playoff drought. Buffalo hadn't played in a postseason game since the 1999 season, and by 2007 patience was starting to wear a little thin.

Maybe a change of venue and time were needed. Monday Night Football games have the football spotlight to themselves at the end of the football work week, and this particular version offered the chance to show the nation that the Bills still could be relevant. It was their first home appearance on a Monday night in 13 years.

They were playing the Dallas Cowboys, which had won its first four games and averaged 38 points per game in the process. The Bills were 1–3, and only had one winning season since 2000. The team's defense was quite battered only a month into the season. Their starting quarterback for this game was rookie Trent Edwards, who had only one start (a win against the Jets) under his professional belt. He moved into the lineup when J.P. Losman suffered a sprained knee.

"Trent's the guy playing this week, and we hope he does an unbelievable job and he gives us a chance to win the game," Bills head coach Dick Jauron said. "And then we'll see what happens."

After this game, maybe patience had run out. The Bills did everything right, and—somehow, some way—everything came out wrong.

It took less than six minutes for the list of unusual events from this game to begin. George Wilson intercepted Tony Romo's overthrown pass and went 25 yards for a touchdown. Romo made up for that mistake early in the second period with a

There was no catching Terrence McGee on this kickoff return.
CREDIT GETTY IMAGES

George Wilson of the Bills and Tony Romo of the Cowboys had many ups and downs in their 2007 matchup.

CREDIT GETTY IMAGES

scoring pass, but the Bills regained the lead via Rian Lindell's short field goal.

Eleven seconds later, Romo's pass from his own end zone was batted into the air and caught by defensive lineman Chris Kelsay for an instant touchdown. The Bills found themselves up by a score of 17–7 on their second pick-six of the night.

Nick Folk capped a drive at the end of the first half with a field goal, and he added three more points early in the third quarter for Dallas. But Terrence McGee—perhaps the best kickoff returner in the history of the Bills—returned the ensuing kickoff 103 yards for a score. Buffalo had a 24–13 lead at the end of the third quarter, even though its offense hadn't anything to do with its three touchdowns.

BOX SCORE

	1ST	2ND	3RD	4TH	FINAL
DALLAS (W, 5-0)	0	10	3	12	25
BUFFALO (L, 1-4)	7	10	7	0	24

SCORING SUMMARY:

QTR	TEAM	PLAY
1ST	BUF.	Wilson 25-yard interception return (Lindell kick)
2ND	DAL.	Romo 22-yard pass to Witten (Folkkick)
2ND	BUF.	Lindell 24-yard field goal
2ND	BUF.	Kelsay interception in end zone (Lindell kick)
2ND	DAL.	Folk 47-yard field goal
3RD	DAL.	Folk 29-yard field goal
3RD	BUF.	McGee 103-yard kickoff return (Lindell kick)
4TH	DAL.	Folk 37-yard field goal
4TH	DAL.	Romo 4-yard pass to Crayton (pass failed)
4TH	DAL.	Folk 53-yard field goal

ATTENDANCE: 71,575

"That really helped us out," McGee said. "I especially wanted to get something started on special teams because it's been a while since I got into the end zone."

Folk's third field goal reduced the margin to eight points early in the fourth quarter. From there it was a matter of seeing if the Bills could hold on. Buffalo couldn't add to its lead in the fourth quarter, and needed one last big defensive play in the final three minutes and 45 seconds. The Cowboys finally found the end zone with 20 seconds left on a short pass from Romo to Patrick Crayton to narrow the lead to 24–22.

Then came an attempted two-point conversion, and the Cowboys failed on it. Romo's pass to wide receiver Terrell Owens was broken up by cornerback Jabari Greer. The exhale by team and fans must have been audible throughout the stadium, and victory for the Bills seemed almost a certainty. All that needed to be done was to recover the obvious onside kick attempt by Folk.

But . . . they couldn't do it. Folk's kick went past the first wave of Bills' receivers due to a missed block, and it was recovered by Dallas' Tony Curtis on the Buffalo 47. Three plays later, Folk lined up for a 53-yard field goal. The kick was up and good, but the Bills had called timeout shortly before the snap. So Folk, now warmed up and confident from his practice kick, simply did it again. Dallas had stolen a win from the Bills, 25–24.

"We felt like we gave a great effort out there, even though it wasn't enough," Greer said. "Dallas came and they made one more play than we did. They fought back and they never quit. Hats off to them."

Ranked No. 29 of 50 by the authors.

NOTEWORTHY: *The Bills had fewer first downs (24 to 14) and total yardage (385 to 229). Marshawn Lynch led Buffalo's offense with 66 yards rushing on 20 carries. Kelsay intercepted three passes in his career, but this was the only one that resulted in a touchdown. Folk's game-winning kick was the longest of his career at that point, and was his first game-winning field goal in the NFL. Ex-Bills coach Wade Phillips returned to Buffalo as the head coach of the Cowboys. His son, Wes, served as one of his assistants. Wes Phillips was a standout player during his years at Williamsville North High School.*

David Nelson's touchdown reception capped Buffalo's win.
CREDIT GETTY IMAGES

SEPTEMBER 18, 2011

RAIDERS At BILLS

IN THE BILLS' long playoff drought at the start of the 21st century, there weren't too many great moments. Some of them, though, were provided by quarterback Ryan Fitzpatrick, who was one of the few Harvard graduates who could be described as a "plucky underdog" upon entering the "real world."

Fitzpatrick had been a reserve for four seasons before signing with the Bills in 2009 as the projected back-up to Trent Edwards. He started three games due to an injury to Edwards, and then later in the season he took over as the full-time starter. Fitzpatrick was 4–4 as the Bills' starting quarterback that year.

He began the 2010 season as Edwards' back-up again under new coach Chan Gailey, but a 0–2 start convinced the coaching staff to elevate Fitz to the starting role. He remained the starter throughout that season, and began the 2011 season as the unquestioned No. 1 at the position. The Bills began the season with a bang in a surprising 41–7 win at Kansas City.

The biggest problem for Fitzpatrick was his inconsistency, going from great to poor in moments. When the Bills played their home opener against Oakland, both sides of Fitzpatrick's play were on display.

The Raiders scored first, early in the second quarter, with a short touchdown run by Michael Bush. Three plays later the Bills set up Oakland's next touchdown with a Fitzpatrick interception. Five plays later, McFadden scored from the 5-yard line and Oakland was in front 14–0.

Buffalo responded with a field goal drive, but many fans were upset with Gailey as he opted for three points instead of going for it on fourth and one from the Raiders' 6-yard line. Oakland's offense was gashing the Bills' porous defense and tacked on another touchdown with three chunk plays that set up Jason Campbell's 1-yard sneak. After a blocked field goal attempt, the Bills were trailing 21–3 at halftime.

Gailey's message to the team at the half was simple: "If they can score that many, we can. Just go stop them and go score three touchdowns and you win 24–21."

Buffalo looked like a completely different team when it came out for the second half. In three plays after intermission, the Bills offense covered 80 yards with running back Fred Jackson going the final 43 for a touchdown.

Then linebacker Nick Barnett forced a McFadden fumble that Dave Batten recovered on the Buffalo 43-yard line. Fitzpatrick quickly turned that into another touchdown on a 7-yard scoring strike to Stevie Johnson. Suddenly the Bills were back in the game, trailing only 21–17 late in the third quarter.

The fourth quarter turned into a table tennis match. The Bills took the lead early in the quarter on a 1-yard run by Jackson. Campbell replied as he threw a touchdown pass to Darren McFadden. Not to be outdone, Fitzpatrick answered with a nine-play, 80-yard drive in four and half minutes that was capped by a touchdown pass to tight end Scott Chandler. Campbell again led Oakland back on a 50-yard scoring play to Denarius Moore. The Raiders had regained the lead, 35–31, with less than four minutes remaining.

There's some debate about when the concept of "Fitzmagic" was born in Western New York, but it is a good way to describe what happened next. The former Ivy League quarterback completed seven of 12 passes and drove the Bills to Oakland's 6. They faced a fourth down and one with 18 seconds left. Fitzpatrick found David Nelson in the end zone for the go-ahead touchdown.

But there was still time left. Campbell navigated the Raiders into position for a Hail Mary pass into the end zone as time expired, but Bills safety Da'Norris Searcy intercepted the pass to secure the Bills' come-from-behind victory. "I had the best view of the ball over everybody," Searcy said. "Once the ball started coming down, I just went up over everybody so I was the first guy to actually touch the ball."

It was a fitting climax to a game that seemed to become more and more exciting as it went on. The two teams combined for 355 yards and 24 first downs in the fourth quarter alone.

"He's a winning quarterback," Gailey said about Fitzpatrick." I don't know if you can give a higher compliment than to say you're a winning quarterback. . . . I'm glad he's on our side."

Ranked No. 24 of 50 by the authors.

BOX SCORE

	1st	2nd	3rd	4th	Final
OAKLAND (L, 1-1)	0	21	0	14	35
BUFFALO (W, 2-0)	0	3	14	21	38

SCORING SUMMARY:

QTR	TEAM	PLAY
2nd	OAK.	Bush 1-yard run (Janikowski kick)
2nd	OAK.	McFadden 5-yard run (Janikowski kick)
2nd	BUF.	Lindell 25-yard field goal
2nd	OAK.	Campbell 1-yard run (Janikowski kick)
3rd	BUF.	Jackson 43-yard run (Lindell kick)
3rd	BUF.	Fitzpatrick 7-yard pass to Johnson (Lindell kick)
4th	BUF.	Jackson 1-yard run (Lindell kick)
4th	OAK.	Campbell 12-yard pass to McFadden (Janikowski kick)
4th	BUF.	Fitzpatrick 6-yard pass to Chandler (Lindell kick)
4th	OAK.	Campbell 50-yard pass to Moore (Janikowski kick)
4th	BUF.	Fitzpatrick 6-yard pass to Nelson (Lindell kick)

ATTENDANCE: 68,191

NOTEWORTHY: *The Bills scored on all five of their second-half offensive possessions. According to the NFL no team in at least 18 years had played such a flawless second half. The 35 points were the second most the Bills ever scored in a second half. Fitzpatrick completed 28 of 46 passes for 264 yards and three touchdowns. Nelson caught 10 passes for 83 yards, both career highs, and Johnson caught eight passes for 96 yards. The Bills set a team record with 34 first downs. The team compiled 481 yards of total offense and averaged 6.8 yards per play.*

SEPTEMBER 25, 2011

PATRIOTS At BILLS

TWICE A YEAR when the Bills played the Patriots early in the 21st century, the same question was asked in Western New York: "When are the Bills ever going to beat those guys again?"

It was a fair question. Buffalo came into the game having lost 20 of 21 games to the Patriots. If not for a 31–0 win on September 7, 2003, the Bills would have broken their own futility record against a single opponent—20 losses in a row to Miami in the 1970's. There was nothing to suggest that New England's 2011 visit would be any different. The Patriots were undefeated and had won 16 of their last 18 regular-season games.

The formula for a Buffalo victory, then, was more or less the standard blueprint. "They're very good about protecting the ball on offense, and they're good at taking it away on defense," Bills quarterback Ryan Fitzpatrick said. "So winning the turnover battle is going to be key for us."

This game began like so many Patriots games had before it. By the second quarter, Tom Brady had thrown three touchdown passes to give New England a 21–0 lead. Same old, same old. Right? But this Buffalo team was more resilient than a Bills squad had been in a long time. The come-from-behind win over the Raiders the week before gave the players confidence that they could rally.

Buffalo's next drive began at their own 4-yard line, Fitzpatrick needed only seven plays to move down the field and score on a pass to Stevie Johnson. An interception by Buffalo's Bryan Scott led to a Rian Lindell field goal. Those 10 points gave

the Bills some hope for the second half.

On the Patriots' first possession of the second half, Leodis McKelvin intercepted Brady and returned it 21 yards to the New England 39-yard line. Fitzpatrick made the Patriots pay for that turnover with a touchdown pass to Scott Chandler. New England responded with a field goal to make it a 24–17 game entering the fourth quarter. The Bills tied the game on a short run by Fred Jackson.

BOX SCORE

	1ST	2ND	3RD	4TH	FINAL
NEW ENGLAND (L, 2-1)	14	7	3	7	31
BUFFALO (W, 3-0)	0	10	7	17	34

SCORING SUMMARY:

QTR	TEAM	PLAY
1ST	N.E.	Brady 14-yard pass to Welker (Gostkowski kick)
1ST	N.E.	Brady 1-yard pass to Gronkowski (Gostkowski kick)
2ND	N.E.	Brady 26-yard pass to Gronkowski (Gostkowski kick)
2ND	BUF.	Fitzpatrick 11-yard pass to Johnson (Lindell kick)
2ND	BUF.	Lindell 42-yard field goal
3RD	BUF.	Fitzpatrick 3-yard pass to Chandler (Lindell kick)
3RD	N.E.	Gostkowski 23-yard field goal
4TH	BUF.	Jackson 1-yard run (Lindell kick)
4TH	BUF.	Florence 27-yard interception return (Lindell kick)
4TH	N.E.	Brady 6-yard pass to Welker (Gostkowski kick)
4TH	BUF.	Lindell 28-yard field goal

ATTENDANCE: 68,174

Following the kickoff, Brady threw his fourth interception of the game (tying a career high), a pass that deflected off the helmet of defensive tackle Marcell Dareus into the hands of cornerback Drayton Florence. The defensive back weaved his way through a number of would-be tacklers to score the go-ahead touchdown. The Bills had taken an almost miraculous 31–24 lead.

"We did talk about the short balls; if we get our hands up we can deflect them," linebacker Nick Barnett said. "They're content in dinking, and that makes plays if you can complete 'em and it's just as good as a run game. That's what we expressed early in the week."

Brady answered with a long drive that he finished off with a tying touchdown pass to Wes Welker. The Bills received the ensuing kickoff with 3:25 remaining. Could Fitz summon some more of his Magic to pull this game out?

The Harvard quarterback went right to work and put together a nice drive to reach the Patriots' 1.

Now the two coaches played a cat-and-mouse game. New England was willing to surrender a touchdown, with the idea it would get the ball back with about 90 seconds remaining—plenty of time for Brady to engineer a tying score. But Gailey instructed Fitzpatrick to sneak the ball but not to score and force New England to use its timeouts.

Fred Jackson had 161 yards of offense and a touchdown for the Bills.
CREDIT GETTY IMAGES

Buffalo ran the clock down to a point when only three seconds remained while Patriots head coach Bill Belichick fumed on the sidelines, probably yelling all sorts of expletives. Lindell booted the winning 28-yard field goal for the improbable 34–31 Bills victory. Buffalo was 3–0 and alone in first place in the AFC East.

"It's time for those past Buffalo Bill memories to fade away," said Florence. "This is a new era, a new day. . . . Everybody outside of this room is calling this an upset, but in this locker room, this is what we expected."

To put this one into perspective, no NFL team since at least 1950 had rallied from 18-point deficits in back-to-back weeks to earn victories . . . until the Bills did it.

"It was awesome to run up the tunnel, looking up at the fans," defensive end Chris Kelsay said. "Ruben Brown was in the tunnel. I played with Ruben the first time we beat them my rookie year [2003] and the last time we beat them until today. . . . I went up to Chan and Buddy (Nix) after the game and said, 'I'm not one to ask for much, but your 24-hour rule (on celebrating wins) I might ask for a couple more hours to enjoy this one—26, 28 hours—because it's been a long time."

Ranked No. 15 of 50 by the authors.

NOTEWORTHY: *Fitzpatrick passed for 369 yards on 27 of 40 passes. Donald Jones caught five passes for 101 yards, Johnson chipped in 94 yards on eight receptions, and Nelson contributed 84 yards on six catches. Jackson rushed for 74 yards and caught passes for another 87.*

ONE BILLS DRIVE

SEPTEMBER 29, 2013

RAVENS At BILLS

A **NEW COACH** always serves as a boost in morale for players and fans alike. In the Bills' case, the team and its followers were hoping that Doug Marrone could change the path of the franchise—one which had put the Bills out of the playoffs for more than a decade at this point.

Marrone's arrival hadn't changed the trajectory of the team through three games. Buffalo dropped two out of three, and the prospects of changing course weren't too great on September 29. The Baltimore Ravens—also known as the defending Super Bowl champions—arrived after winning two of their first three.

It would be difficult to beat the Ravens under most circumstances, but this was a day when the Bills' defenders committed larceny on several occasions and thus stole a win.

Who says crime does not pay?

The Bills started the game slowly but efficiently. Dan Carpenter kicked two field goals, both from 27 yards, to take the early lead. The idea was to control the football, and Buffalo did exactly that in the early going. "Our game plan was to come into this game running the ball, a lot of double tight ends and fullback," wide receiver Robert Woods said. "Just to play a powerful football game, play physical with a physical team—I think we did that, did great on the ground."

Baltimore countered early in the second period as Joe Flacco threw a 10-yard touchdown pass to Marlon Brown after rookie E.J.

Bills' defensive back Aaron Williams makes an acrobatic interception.
CREDIT GETTY IMAGES

Manuel's lost fumble deep in his own territory. But Buffalo had a speedy answer, scoring two touchdowns in less than two minutes. Woods' 42-yard pass from Manuel was the more spectacular play, but Fred Jackson's gallop up the middle counted just as much on the scoreboard. The Bills took a 20–7 lead into halftime.

Flacco moved the Ravens closer about midway through the third quarter with a 26-yard TD pass to Torrey Smith. But Carpenter responded with a short field goal about five minutes later to put the Bills up by nine again.

There were no more touchdowns for the rest of the day, but that doesn't mean there wasn't much drama. Tucker kicked a 35-yard field goal with 7:12 left to put the Ravens within one possession, and a defensive stand and a long pass put Baltimore in business on the Buffalo 11. Mario Williams' sack helped stall the drive, and the Ravens settled for a Tucker field goal that cut the margin to 23–20 with 4:04 left. When Baltimore regained possession of the ball with 2:20 to go, it was easy to wonder if the Bills could hang on.

"We all felt that way at the end," Ravens coach John Harbaugh said. "I felt like we were going to win the game."

They didn't, thanks in large part to linebacker Kiko Alonso. Flacco tried to pass the ball to Dallas Clark, but Bills safety Da'Norris Searcy deflected it into the waiting hands of Alonso with 57 seconds left. It was the fifth pick by the Bills' defense during the day and the second by Alonso, who also had a sack, a forced fumble, and a fumble recovery in a game that had people talking about his chances to be the NFL's Defensive Rookie of the Year.

"Kiko got a good shot on the tight end [Dallas Clark] near the line of scrimmage to slow him down and he got him off his route," Searcy said. "So when Flacco threw it, I broke on it. I tried to reach around him and catch it but I ended up tipping it. I saw Kiko dive over me and intercept it. Great play by Kiko."

Buffalo escaped with a 23–20 victory, and Flacco felt responsible. "Things were going our way a lot, just not when I threw it to them," Flacco said. "We had four interceptions and still had a chance to win at the end. With the way I played, turning the ball over and all that, the fact that we were able to hang in there and still have a shot at the end, we did certain things well."

Ranked No. 50 of 50 by the authors.

BOX SCORE

	1ST	2ND	3RD	4TH	FINAL
BALTIMORE (L, 2-2)	0	7	7	6	20
BUFFALO (W, 2-2)	6	14	3	0	23

SCORING SUMMARY:

QTR	TEAM	PLAY
1ST	BUF.	Carpenter 27-yard field goal
1ST	BUF.	Carpenter 27-yard field goal
2ND	BAL.	Flacco 10-yard pass to Brown (Tucker kick)
2ND	BUF.	Manuel 42-yard pass to Woods (Carpenter kick)
2ND	BUF.	Jackson 16-yard run (Carpenter kick)
3RD	BAL.	Flacco 26-yard pass to Smith (Tucker kick)
3RD	BUF.	Carpenter 22-yard field goal
4TH	BAL.	Tucker 35-yard field goal
4TH	BAL.	Tucker 24-yard field goal

ATTENDANCE: 68,296

NOTEWORTHY: *It was the first time since 1996 that the Bills had defeated a defending Super Bowl champion (Dallas). Manuel only threw 22 passes, but the Bills did run for 203 yards to help give them a good-sized edge in the time of possession. The 55 rushing attempts allowed were a franchise record for the Ravens. Aaron Williams had two interceptions for the Bills, while Jim Leonhard also grabbed one. The teams were a combined 8 of 34 on third-down conversions. The Bills did not give up a rushing first down in the game. Buffalo had not scored in the first quarter all season until Carpenter's first field goal.*

DECEMBER 10, 2017

COLTS At BILLS

CONSIDERING the location of the Bills' home in Orchard Park—smack in the middle of the predominant snowbelt in the region—and Buffalo's reputation for frosty flakes in the winter, it's a little surprising that the team hasn't played many home games in heavy snowstorms over the years.

This was the biggest exception.

Clouds started dumping precipitation on the area surrounding New Era Field about 30 minutes before the opening kickoff, and it didn't stop until well after the game . . . gaining momentum as the afternoon went along. About eight inches of snow fell during the contest, accompanied by some cold winds. Twenty men were given blowers so that the yard-lines and the hashmarks on the field could be cleared off during each break of the game. In other words, it was a mess.

"I've never played in the snow in my life, let alone those conditions out there," Bills defensive end Ryan Davis said. "When we came out for warmups, I immediately did a snow angel."

Even so, Buffalo's fans turned out for the game. Most of the lower bowl of the stadium was filled, even if it meant standing on a snowbank while watching the contest. How much the fans actually saw depended on the seat location, but the white-out conditions certainly caused some to listen to the public-address announcer to hear what had happened in a given play. And with the Colts dressed in all-white—pants, jerseys and helmets—it was almost impossible to decipher the Indianapolis players' identities.

"I want to say that our fans and the people here are the toughest damn people in the world," Bills' defensive tackle Kyle Williams said. "They deserve as much credit as anybody, and I love being here. I love playing for those guys."

The conditions meant that it was going to be an unusual day for football, but that didn't lessen the importance of the game to the Bills. Buffalo was 6–6 entering the contest, which put the team right in the middle of the playoff race. Buffalo had lost four of its last five, and couldn't afford a loss to the lowly Colts.

Offense figured to be a problem for the Bills entering the game, as starter Tyrod Taylor was injured and couldn't play. That left backup Nathan Peterman as the team's best hope. He'd try to lead the offense on a day when it was tough to run and almost impossible to throw.

Everyone had an idea what the day would be like by the first quarter. No one scored, and the two teams combined for all of nine passing yards. The only scoring opportunity came when Adam Vinatieri attempted a 33-yard field goal for the Colts. It didn't come close to passing through the uprights.

Deonte Thompson's amazing catch led to the Bills' overtime win.
CREDIT-GETTY IMAGES

Late in the second quarter, Buffalo finally had a solid drive. LeSean McCoy led the way with a couple of good-sized runs, and Peterman threw to Kelvin Benjamin for a touchdown. It was the first time Peterman had played in a game in which his Bills' team had the lead.

The young quarterback didn't have time to enjoy the look of the scoreboard. He suffered a head injury in the third quarter. That brought in Joe Webb, the team's emergency QB, to take over. Still, it looked like the 7–0 lead would hold up. But in the fourth quarter, the Colts went on a long drive that took almost 10 minutes. It ended with a touchdown pass by Jacoby Brissett on an option play.

The Colts converted a two-point play to take the lead, but they were called for pass interference. That meant Vinatieri needed to kick a 43-yard extra point simply to tie the game. Vinatieri, one of the greatest clutch kickers of his generation, made it. It might have been the kick of his lifetime. "I swear that ball was not going in. It just got up in the wind and it just curved right in," Bills safety Micah Hyde said about the "banana ball" of a kick.

Finally and mercifully, the game ended when McCoy dashed for the winning touchdown with only 1:33 left in overtime. He went through a hole and found himself in open space in the secondary. The rest was easy. Bills' guard Richie Incognito said it was a simple play call: "Run right behind Richie." The touchdown was set up by an incredible third-down catch by Deonte Thompson on a pass from Webb that turned into a 34-yard gain. The game's conclusion was celebrated by a good-natured snowball fight among the Bills' players as fans threw snow in the air.

The win kept Buffalo's playoff hopes alive . . . once the team thawed out of course. Ask rookie Tre'Davious White, who had never played in snow before.

"I was ready to get inside," he said.

As was everyone else.

Ranked No. 11 of 50 by the authors.

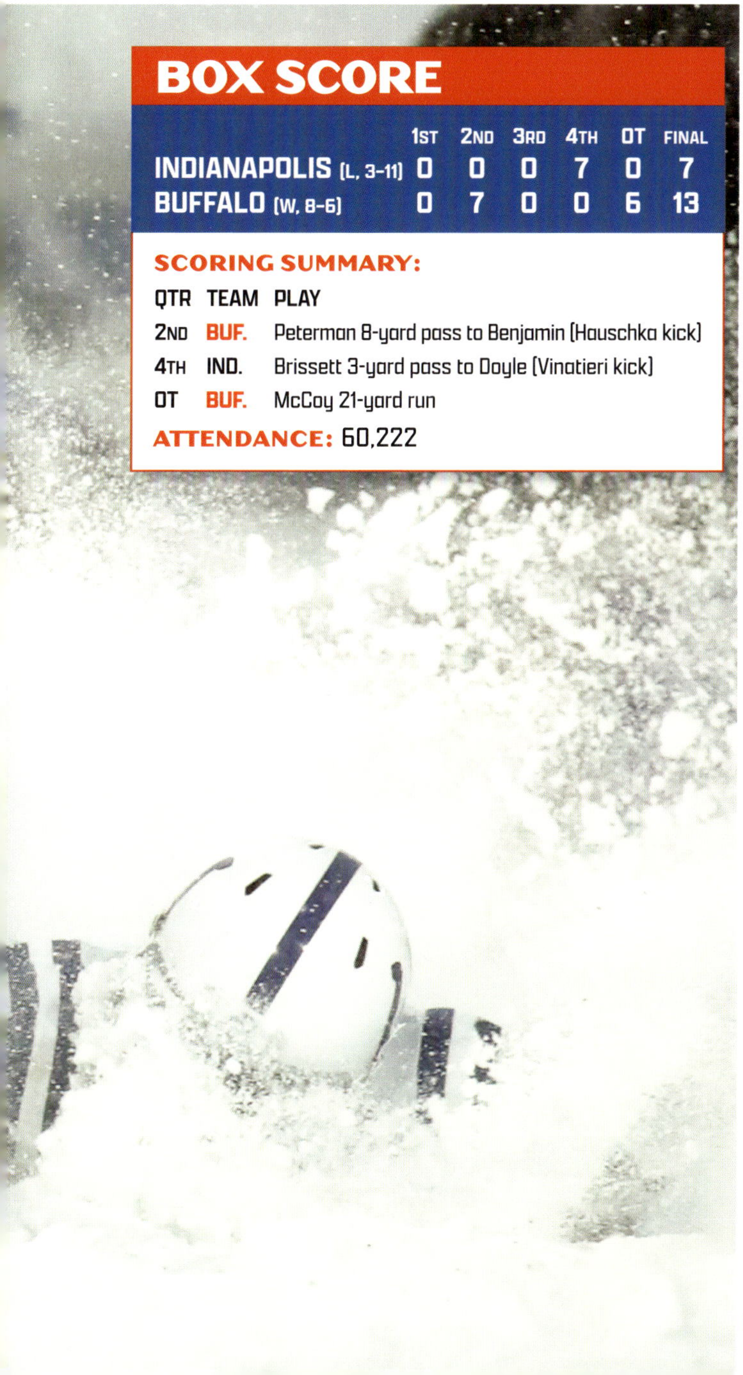

BOX SCORE

	1ST	2ND	3RD	4TH	OT	FINAL
INDIANAPOLIS (L, 3-11)	0	0	0	7	0	7
BUFFALO (W, 8-6)	0	7	0	0	6	13

SCORING SUMMARY:

QTR	TEAM	PLAY
2ND	BUF.	Peterman 8-yard pass to Benjamin (Hauschka kick)
4TH	IND.	Brissett 3-yard pass to Doyle (Vinatieri kick)
OT	BUF.	McCoy 21-yard run

ATTENDANCE: 60,222

NOTEWORTHY: *Running backs McCoy of the Bills and Frank Gore of the Colts were two of the few stand-outs on offense. McCoy ran 32 times for 156 yards, while Gore went 36 times for 130 yards. Neither team had 100 yards passing. The Bills had the only two turnovers of the game, an interception and a fumble.*

Tyler Kroft snags one of two touchdown passes on the day.
CREDIT GETTY IMAGES

ONE BILLS DRIVE

SEPTEMBER 27, 2020

RAMS At BILLS

NO ONE EVER thought that attendance at a Buffalo Bills' home game would be zero. Then again, no one ever thought a pandemic would shut down so much of our lives.

The COVID-19 virus arrived early in 2020, sending most of the major sports teams in North America into hibernation. The National Football League did have the advantage over the other leagues of having a regular season that began in September. That gave the NFL time to figure out how to stage its schedule.

The league essentially put the teams into quarantine, testing everyone regularly and isolating anyone who had come into contact with the virus. It also cancelled all preseason games, but the regular season began as planned. The catch came with the fact that New York State was not ready to allow any fans into the building under any circumstances. Thus a stadium that usually seats more than 70,000 was empty for the home opener against the New York Jets.

"Obviously it's going to be different, but I've still got to play the game," safety Jordan Poyer said before that game.

The Bills beat the Jets on September 13, and then won in Miami a week later. That brought the team back to Bills Stadium for a game with the Los Angeles Rams. Even if there was still no "studio audience" for the game, the teams put on a terrific show for those watching on television at home.

The Bills played the first half like they were on a mission to show to the rest of the league that they were a Super Bowl contender. Following an even first quarter where the Bills took an early 7–0 lead on a 1-yard reception by tight end Lee Smith, Buffalo scored twice more in the second quarter. Allen scored on a 1-yard run and then—following a Rams field goal—Allen tossed a 3-yard scoring pass to tight end Tyler Kroft.

The Bills' quarterback gave himself a halftime pep talk, saying, "I can't let this team get back in the game. It can't be me. They've got to earn it."

The Bills took a commanding 25-point lead early in the third quarter with Allen's third touchdown pass. However, from there the quarterback forgot his own advice to himself. After the Rams had cut Buffalo's lead to 28–10, Allen threw an ill-advised pass to Kroft, and Rams safety John Johnson swiped the ball out of the receiver's grasp. Three plays later, former Bill Robert Woods caught a 25-yard touchdown pass, and Los Angeles was back in the game with plenty of time left.

The Rams had seized the momentum, and Jared Goff then engineered a 97-yard touchdown drive. With a successful two-point conversion, LA was down by only three points.

Allen made another miscue and then compounded it. The Rams' all-everything defensive end Aaron Donald sacked Allen, forced a fumble, and recovered it. Allen received an unsportsmanlike conduct penalty for protesting the call, and LA was in business in Buffalo territory. Six players later the Rams were in the lead, 32–28.

Allen composed himself and steered the Bills 75 yards in 11 plays. The drive ended when he found Kroft open in the end zone from three yards out for the game-winning touchdown with 15 seconds left. The only noise in the stadium was the screaming by Bills players, which was duplicated by the many thousands of fans whose cheering could only be heard in their homes. The Bills overcame third-and-22 and third-and-25 situations on the game-winning drive.

"Holy cow," center Mitch Morse said. "You talk about a guy, when he scored the touchdown, our sideline erupted. It's fun to see him score, because he's the best guy. He's the best dude."

"For a guy like Tyler, who hasn't played a whole lot," Allen said, "we haven't asked a bunch of our tight ends, to kind of step in and catch two touchdown catches for us. . . . This team is just made up of selfless guys that are just trying to do their job when their number's called. And that's why we love being a part of it and that's why this team loves each other."

Ranked No. 44 of 50 by the authors.

BOX SCORE

	1ST	2ND	3RD	4TH	FINAL
L.A. RAMS (L, 2-1)	0	3	14	15	32
BUFFALO (W, 3-0)	7	14	7	7	35

SCORING SUMMARY:

QTR	TEAM	PLAY
1ST	BUF.	Allen 1-yard pass to Smith (Bass kick)
2ND	BUF.	Allen 1-yard run (Bass kick)
2ND	LAR.	Sloman 30-yard field goal
2ND	BUF.	Allen 3-yard pass to Kroft (Bass kick)
3RD	BUF.	Allen 4-yard pass to Diggs (Bass kick)
3RD	LAR.	Goff 1-yard run (Sloman kick)
3RD	LAR.	Goff 25-yard pass to Woods (Sloman kick)
4TH	LAR.	Goff 16-yard pass to Kupp (Goff pass to Higbee)
4TH	LAR.	Henderson 1-yard run (Sloman kick)
4TH	BUF.	Allen 3-yard pass to Kroft (Bass kick)

ATTENDANCE: 0 (COVID restrictions)

NOTEWORTHY: *Smith's touchdown catch was his first play of the season. He had replaced Dawson Knox who was out of the lineup with a concussion. Smith also had caught a touchdown pass against the Rams the last time they were in Orchard Park, back in 2012. Allen completed 24 of 33 passes for 311 yards with four touchdowns and one interception. He was the first Bills quarterback since Jim Kelly in 1992 to have three consecutive games with more than 300 yards passing and his 1,050 yards passing in the first three games of a season was the most ever by a Bill. The Bills defense allowed 28 first downs and 478 yards.*

JANUARY 9, 2021

COLTS At BILLS

THERE WAS something different about the game played in Bills Stadium when the playoffs opened compared to the regular season contests in 2020: fans.

Those earlier games were played without people in the stands, due to COVID-19 restrictions. But when the playoffs arrived in January, team and civic officials worked out a complicated formula that would allow a limited number of people to watch. They were socially distanced in groups of two or four, and scattered around the building. But they were there.

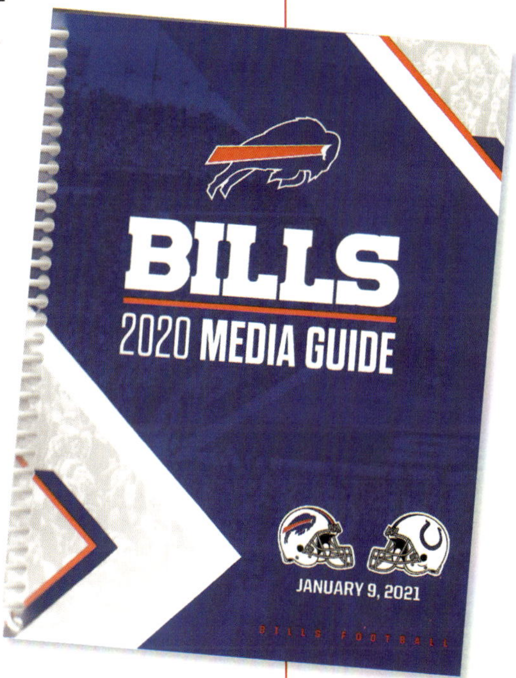

About 6,800 season-ticket holders, family members and sponsors attended the game, which was the first playoff contest in the stadium in 8,778 days. The last time the Bills hosted a playoff game was December 28, 1996. The fans had passed COVID-19 tests within 72 hours of the opening kickoff, and presented proof of the result before they were allowed into the building.

"I'm sure if it could be 200,000, there'd be 200,000 in the stands," safety Jordan Poyer said. "It's a step in the right direction. We know they're excited. We know they want to be at the games."

The Bills came into the game on a major roll, having won their final six games—all by at least 10 points. The last three victories were by margins of 29, 29 and 30 points. The Colts were hardly slackers, finishing an 11–6 season by going 4–1 down the stretch. Indianapolis must have figured that stopping the league's passing combination—Josh Allen to Stefon Diggs—was a must.

This would be the first time Diggs had played in a home game as a Bill with fans in the stadium. The veteran even played catch with a few of the fans before the game, as he had done throughout his pro career. "I wish there were some more kids out there," he said. "I only got some adults, so I've got to work on my arm, but it was definitely a hell of a time and I look forward to doing it again."

The Colts took the early lead with a field goal, but the Bills answered on a short touchdown pass from Allen to Dawson Knox. The play was set up by a 36-yard pass to Diggs. The Colts needed about 10 minutes to respond, but eventually Jonathan Taylor plunged into the end zone to give Indianapolis a three-point lead.

The Colts had a big chance to increase their lead later in the quarter, having the ball first-and-goal on the Buffalo 4, but a fourth-down gamble left them empty. "I think the turning point of the game was that fourth-and-goal stop by our defense," Allen said. The Bills still had time to answer, and did so

Only 6,800 fans were allowed in the stands for this playoff game with Indianapolis.
CREDIT GETTY IMAGES

with a 96-yard drive that included two good-sized passes to Gabriel Davis. Allen eventually ran it in to give the Bills the lead.

Buffalo opened the third quarter with the ball, and padded the lead to 17–10 on Tyler Bass's field goal. Soon after that, the Bills pulled off the biggest play of the game. Allen's long pass down the sideline beat a blitz and was caught by Diggs, who ran it home for a touchdown. "I've been begging for that play for a while," Allen said. "He [offensive coordinator Brian Daboll] called it in the perfect opportunity, the perfect situation."

Yet the Colts weren't through. Two long runs helped set up a touchdown pass by Rivers to cut the margin to 24–16. Buffalo responded with a 54-

BOX SCORE

	1ST	2ND	3RD	4TH	FINAL
INDIANAPOLIS (L)	3	7	0	14	24
BUFFALO (W)	7	7	3	10	27

SCORING SUMMARY:

QTR	TEAM	PLAY
1ST	IND.	Blankenship 30-yard field goal
1ST	BUF.	Allen 3-yard pass to Knox (Bass kick)
2ND	IND.	Taylor 1-yard run (Blankenship kick)
2ND	BUF.	Allen 5-yard run (Bass kick)
3RD	BUF.	Bass 46-yard field goal
4TH	BUF.	Allen 35-yard pass to Diggs (Bass kick)
4TH	IND.	Rivers 9-yard pass to Pascal (run failed)
4TH	BUF.	Bass 54-yard field goal
4TH	IND.	Rivers 27-yard pass to Doyle (Rivers pass to Doyle)

ATTENDANCE: 6,772 (COVID restrictions)

yard field goal by Bass, and the lead was 11 points . . . for about two minutes. Two big plays later, the Colts were only down by a field goal. What's more, the Bills' next drive stalled after a couple of first downs, so Indy had a chance to win the game in the final 2:30.

The Colts did move the ball into Buffalo territory, but they weren't close enough to consider kicking a tying field goal. After three straight incompletions—including a last-ditch long pass that was knocked down by safety Micah Hyde—the Bills had wrapped up the win and a ticket to the divisional round of the playoffs.

It had never been easy. When it was over, the Bills could finally share a win with their fans, who had been watching faithfully but relatively silently at home during the regular season.

"You could feel it in the air," Bills coach Sean McDermott said. "Just the atmosphere and the environment—[it] was almost like it was full, especially down the stretch there. Just special. Only in Buffalo."

Ranked No. 45 of 50 by the authors.

NOTEWORTHY: *It was the Bills' first win of a playoff game in 25 years. Indianapolis lost in the first round of the postseason for the first time since 2012. The Colts rolled up 472 yards of total offense in the game, including 163 on the ground. Buffalo wasn't too far behind at 397. Buffalo's 96-yard drive was the longest in the team's playoff history at that point. It was also the only drive of that length to take less than two minutes in NFL playoff history. Allen became the fifth NFL quarterback since 1940 to have a touchdown running, passing and receiving in the playoffs.*

ONE BILLS DRIVE

AFC PLAYOFFS

JANUARY 16, 2021

RAVENS At BILLS

IT'S INTERESTING that in an extremely complicated game like professional football, public attention quickly narrows down to the quarterbacks. They are usually credited with the wins and blamed for the losses. When two good ones are matched in the postseason, the attention level on them seems to grow exponentially.

This playoff game between the Bills and Ravens certainly had that. Buffalo's Josh Allen had taken a major step forward in his third season in the league, piling up career bests in touchdown passes and passing yards. Meanwhile, Lamar Jackson of Baltimore had taken his play to a high level in 2019, winning the league's Most Valuable Player award. He was great in the 2020 season, too.

There were questions about both of them entering the pros, even though they were both first-round draft choices. They had answered all of them by gametime. "They've come up on the quote-unquote other side of the tracks from a football perspective where they came up the hard way, doubted often, and had to overcome that," Ravens' coach John Harbaugh said. "I always like the underdog."

Only about 7,000 people were allowed into Bills Stadium because of pandemic restrictions this day. But everyone—especially the television executives at NBC—was hoping for an offensive explosion led by the two stars. Alas, that never happened. Even so, there were a couple of moments in the game that turned out to be memorable in very different ways.

Neither of them came in the quiet first half. The Ravens set the tone by taking the opening kickoff and staging an eight-minute drive that ended with a missed field goal. Buffalo later took advantage of good field position to move into the red zone.

Taron Johnson receives an escort during a spectacular interception return.
CREDIT GETTY IMAGES

There the drive stalled, but Tyler Bass's short field goal put the Bills ahead. The Ravens generated enough offense to score a tying field goal late in the first half.

The Bills figured out how to move the ball at the start of the third quarter. They successfully mixed Allen's passes with some key plays by running back Devin Singletary. Finally and almost inevitably, Allen completed a touchdown pass to Stefon Diggs to take a 10–3 lead. Baltimore answered with a long drive of its own. Eventually, the Ravens reached a third-and-goal at the Buffalo 9. Jackson threw a short pass over the middle that was intended for tight end Mark Andrews at the goal line.

However, the ball wound up in the hands of defensive back Taron Johnson of the Bills, who cut in front of the receiver. Johnson was a yard into the end zone, and made the quick decision to run the ball the other way rather than taking the safe touchback.

"I caught the ball and kind of looked down, but then I looked up and saw a whole bunch of green grass to that side of me," Johnson said. "At that point, there's one person I have to beat. And that's No. 8 [Jackson]."

The decision proved wise. After about 20 yards of broken-field running, Johnson was in open space with a convoy of blockers waiting to assist. He went the distance for the touchdown, a 101-yard interception return. That tied an NFL record for the longest "pick six" in playoff history.

"Taron Johnson's is a play that people are going to remember for a long time here in Buffalo, potentially a franchise-altering play," Allen said.

The Bills had been looking at a tie game late in the third quarter. Instead, they were ahead by 14 points. While every fan in the nation immediately could label the play as a proverbial turning point, they also knew that Jackson was capable of magic. In other words, nothing was settled.

But those fears didn't last long. Jackson was hit on the final play of the third quarter by Buffalo's Tremaine Edmunds and Trent Murphy. The quarterback had to leave the game because of a concussion. Therefore, the Bills had a 17–3 lead, and Tyler Huntley would be the Ravens' quarterback for the rest of the game. The chances of a Baltimore comeback became faint in that instant.

The Bills' offense didn't do much for the rest of the game, picking up only three first downs in the fourth quarter. But the Ravens couldn't reach the end zone in the remaining time, and the Bills were 17–3 winners. The "three" in that score was very significant, since Baltimore was averaging more than 29 points per game . . . and the Bills shut them down.

"Fraz [defensive coordinator Leslie Frazier]and all the coaches put together a game plan that we new could work," safety Micah Hyde said. "Last time we played them, there were five or six plays that we gave them. If we wouldn't have [done that] it would have been a totally different outcome."

It was Buffalo's eighth straight victory, and marked the first time since 1994 that the team had reached the AFC Championship game.

"We're excited," Johnson said. "It's not done yet. We're not done yet. We're trying to get to the big show."

Ranked No. 35 of 50 by the authors.

NOTEWORTHY: *Allen finished the day 23 of 37 with 206 yards and no interceptions. Diggs caught eight of those passes for 106 yards and the score. Johnson's touchdown was the Bills' first by a defensive player in the playoffs since Jeff Burris had one on an interception in 1996 against Jacksonville.*

BOX SCORE

	1ST	2ND	3RD	4TH	FINAL
BALTIMORE (L)	0	3	0	0	3
BUFFALO (W)	3	0	14	0	17

SCORING SUMMARY:

QTR	TEAM	PLAY
1ST	BUF.	Bass 28-yard field goal
2ND	BAL.	Tucker 34-yard field
3RD	BUF.	Allen 3-yard pass to Diggs (Bass kick)
3RD	BUF.	Johnson 101-yard interception return (Bass kick)

ATTENDANCE: 6,772 (COVID-19 restrictions)

JANUARY 15, 2022

PATRIOTS At BILLS

A **PITCHER** can throw a perfect game in baseball, sending 27 straight batters back to the dugout after making an out. A bowler can throw a perfect 300 game by rolling 12 straight strikes. But a unit of a football team can't really have a truly perfect game.

Still, the Bills' offense came as close as possible in its playoff-opening win against the Patriots. Buffalo had the ball seven times when a drive didn't end with a kneel-down. It scored seven touchdowns in the game, giving punter Matt Haack a very unexpected day off. It's the first time that had happened in the Super Bowl era.

"That sounds like some Pop Warner stuff," Bills defensive tackle Harrison Phillips said after the game.

The tone of the contest—the first postseason meeting between the teams in 58 years—was set immediately. Josh Allen threw a pair of touchdown passes to tight end Dawson Knox in a span of a little more than nine minutes of the first quarter. In other words, the Patriots trailed 14–0 before they knew what hit them. Knox became the first Bills' tight end to score two touchdowns in a playoff game. The first one was intended by Allen to be a simple throwaway pass, but Knox caught it anyway. It was one of those nights.

It was no better for the New England offense in the early going. Its first drive ended with safety's Micah Hyde's sensational, over-the-shoulder interception.

"When I knew he was throwing, I just put my head down and started running," Hyde said. "I knew it was going to be at the receiver, and I just looked up at the last second and the ball was there. And so, was able to make a play on it."

"I told him on the sideline, 'That might have been the most unbelievable play I've ever seen on the field," teammate Jordan Poyer said. "... I mean it looked like the receiver had maybe a step, but Micah was there and made an unbelievable play. Like I said, probably one of the best plays I had ever seen on the field."

In the second quarter, the Bills changed their scoring approach. They had a player score two touchdowns again, but this time Devin Singletary did it on runs. Nick Folk of the Patriots had a field goal in the final seconds of the half to spoil the defense's chance at "perfection," but no one on the Buffalo side was complaining about a 27–3 lead at halftime.

The numbers were staggering. The Bills had 300 yards of total offense in the first 30 minutes, and had 19 first downs. "Shoot, every drive we couldn't get a stop was frustrating," New England linebacker Matthew Judon said. "It wasn't only one play. It wasn't one, single player. It was everything. It was the whole game."

The Bills opened the third quarter with their longest touchdown play of the day. Allen completed a 34-yard scoring pass to Emmanuel Sanders. The Patriots finally scored later in the period as Mac

Jones found Kendrick Bourne for a 3-yard touchdown. Still, at 33–10, no one from New England celebrated too much.

Allen stayed on the field long enough to engineer two more passing touchdowns, running his total to five on the day. Gabriel Davis and Tommy Doyle (who usually served as a spare offensive lineman) did the honors. With that, Allen headed to the sidelines and took off his helmet, as backup Mitch Trubisky cleaned up in the final minutes. Jones and Bourne combined for one more touchdown for the Patriots at the end of the game.

Players from both sides of the ball for the Bills had plenty to say later. "I think we feel good," Allen said. "There are some things that we can clean up and work on. But at the end of the day, we moved on, we're on to the next one and it doesn't matter what we did today. It's what we do next week."

"There was a lot of disrespect coming toward our defense. And so we felt like the only way to shut people up is to go out there and play football and let you guys sit and watch and talk," lineman Jerry Hughes said. "And that's what we're doing right now, playing football."

New England head coach Bill Belichick supplied the last words: "We just couldn't keep up with them."

Ranked No. 7 of 50 by the authors.

NOTEWORTHY: *The gametime temperature was 7 degrees, one of the coldest home games in Bills history. Some 30-mile-per-hour winds winds didn't help anyone trying to stay warm either. Buffalo's 30-point win and 47 points scored were second on its all-time record list in those categories. The 1991 win over the Raiders by a score of 51–3 is No. 1 in both categories. Allen finished 21 of 25 for 308 yards.*

BOX SCORE

	1ST	2ND	3RD	4TH	FINAL
NEW ENGLAND (L)	0	3	7	7	17
BUFFALO (W)	14	13	6	14	47

SCORING SUMMARY:

QTR	TEAM	PLAY
1ST	BUF.	Allen 8-yard pass to Knox (Bass kick)
1ST	BUF.	Allen 11-yard pass to Knox (Bass kick)
2ND	BUF.	Singletary 3-yard run (kick failed)
2ND	BUF.	Singletary 16-yard run (Bass kick)
2ND	N.E.	Folk 44-yard field goal
3RD	BUF.	Allen 34-yard pass to Sanders (kick failed)
3RD	N.E.	Jones 3-yard pass to Bourne (Folk kick)
4TH	BUF.	Allen 19-yard pass to Davis (Bass kick)
4TH	BUF.	Allen 1-yard pass to Doyle (Bass kick)
4TH	N.E.	Jones 4-yard pass to Bourne (Folk kick)

ATTENDANCE: 69,188

Micah Hyde's interception set the tone in the win over New England.
CREDIT GETTY IMAGES

ONE BILLS DRIVE

NOVEMBER 13, 2022

VIKINGS At BILLS

SOMETIMES football teams have seasons where everything seems to go right. The ball bounces in their direction, field-goal attempts hit the upright and bounce through, and passes are deflected to someone in the proper colored jersey.

The Minnesota Vikings of 2022 had one of those years. That team was coming off an 8–9 season, and little improvement was expected a year later. Perhaps new coach Kevin O'Connell could change their luck.

After dividing their first two games, the Vikings went on an impressive winning streak before arriving in Buffalo. They had won six games in a row, all by one possession (eight points or fewer). Minnesota had been trailing within the final three minutes four different times in the season already, yet won. The Bills were anxious to see if the Vikings' good fortune would hold up for another week.

Minnesota started the game well enough, as Justin Jefferson caught a touchdown pass early in the first quarter. Jefferson had a Buffalo connection, as the Vikings picked him with the first-round draft choice that the Bills had given up in order to obtain Stefon Diggs. But Buffalo more or less dominated play for the rest of the half. Devin Singletary ran for two scores, Tyler Bass kicked a field goal, and Gabe Davis caught a touchdown pass from Josh Allen. It was 24–10 at halftime, and the game seemed even safer when Bass added another field goal late in the third quarter.

But only 17 seconds after that kick, Dalvin Cook rambled 81 yards for a Minnesota touchdown. The Vikings added another touchdown in the fourth quarter, but a missed

Justin Jefferson's catch for the Vikings may have been the best in the stadium's history.
CREDIT GETTY IMAGES

point after conversion left the score at 27–23. Minnesota had one more drive about three minutes later, and looked destined to take the lead. Jefferson made an unbelievable one-handed catch on a fourth-and-18 play to move into Buffalo territory.

"It felt like it was unreal—like a movie," Jefferson said about a catch that surely ranks as one of the greatest in the stadium's history.

The Vikings moved the ball another 45 or so yards until the Bills had a memorable goal-line stand to stop the Vikings on fourth down inches from the goal line. With only 49 seconds left, a Bills' victory seemed assured. But Allen fumbled the first-down snap from center Mitch Morse, and Eric Kendricks recovered in the end zone for a Minnesota touchdown. It was beyond shocking under the circumstances.

At least the Bills still had some time left on the clock, and Allen deftly moved the ball down the field. When the drive ran out of time, Bass kicked a 29-yard field goal to send the game into overtime.

The Vikings settled for a field goal in the extra period after having a first and goal at the Bills' 2. The Bills defensive stand gave Allen and company a chance to answer. It looked like Buffalo would do just that . . . until Allen's pass was intercepted by Patrick Peterson with only 1:12 left in OT. It was the Bills' fourth turnover of the day, and it finalized the Vikings' 33–30 victory.

From the Buffalo standpoint, it was a great game and a memorable game—perhaps the most exciting game of the NFL season. But it wasn't a win. The defeat knocked the Bills out of the lead in the AFC East, as they fell a half-game behind Miami.

"Horrendous second half," said Allen, who had suffered an elbow injury the previous week but played through some pain. "It comes down to my shoulders and my shoulders only. Making the right decisions, making the right throws."

Meanwhile, the Vikings were still playing as if they had rabbit's feet in their pockets. If anyone questioned their status as a league power, they could simply point to the standings.

"Look at us now. Look at us now. That's all I could say," Peterson said. "We're not trying to prove them [the critics] wrong. We just want to continue to prove ourselves right each and every time we step on the field."

Ranked No. 23 of 50 by the authors.

BOX SCORE

	1st	2nd	3rd	4th	OT	Final
MINNESOTA (W, 8-1)	7	3	7	13	3	33
BUFFALO (L, 6-3)	14	10	3	3	0	30

SCORING SUMMARY:

QTR	TEAM	PLAY
1st	MIN.	Cousins 22-yard pass to Jefferson (Joseph kick)
1st	BUF.	Singletary 5-yard run (Bass kick)
1st	BUF.	Singletary 1-yard run (Bass kick)
2nd	BUF.	Bass 34-yard field goal
2nd	MIN.	Joseph 27-yard field goal
2nd	BUF.	Allen 11-yard pass to Davis (Bass kick)
3rd	BUF.	Bass 45-yard field goal
3rd	MIN.	Cook 81-yard run (Joseph kick)
4th	MIN.	Ham 3-yard run (kick failed)
4th	MIN.	Kendricks fumble recovery in end zone (Joseph kick)
4th	BUF.	Bass 29-yard field goal
OT	MIN.	Joseph 33-yard field goal

ATTENDANCE: 70,844

NOTEWORTHY: *It was the first time the Bills had blown a 14-point halftime lead in their home stadium in Orchard Park. The two quarterbacks ran up some impressive statistics. Allen finished 29 of 43 for 330 yards, while Kirk Cousins was 30 of 50 for 357 yards. Both threw two interceptions. Cook ran for 119 yards on only 14 carries, but that included 81 yards in one gulp. Jefferson had 10 catches for 193 yards, and Diggs had 12 receptions for 128 yards. Diggs also had a terrific one-handed catch late in the third quarter. Brothers Dalvin Cook of the Vikings and James Cook of the Bills swapped jerseys after the game.*

JANUARY 8, 2023

PATRIOTS At BILLS

IT HAD BEEN an exhausting week for the Bills, and they hadn't even played a down yet.

The week before in Cincinnati, defensive back Damar Hamlin delivered a hit on a Bengals' player, paused for a moment, and collapsed. His heart had stopped. Responders resuscitated him right on the turf and rushed him to the University of Cincinnati hospital—where he was initially listed as critical. The game, which at the time was an important matchup between two of the AFC's best, suddenly became immaterial. The contest was cancelled.

But the season must go on, and it did. The New England Patriots were coming to town for the final game of the regular season, no matter how any of the Bills were feeling.

"To him getting up, to him falling, to everything, it's just something that I can't unsee," cornerback Tre'Davious White said. "Every time I close my eyes, it replays. I try watching TV, and every time the TV goes to commercial, it's just the only thing that comes to my mind, just the vision of that. So, it's been a tough week. It's been a tough week for our whole team. But it's not about us right now. It's about Damar and his family, man, and just what they had to go through. . . . And hopefully we'll never have to go through this again."

The good news was that Hamlin recovered quickly and was released from the hospital later in the week. Back in Buffalo, he even figured out a way to show up for the Bills' regular-season finale against New England. The rookie greeted the team in the locker room before the game, and then watched the contest from a suite.

It already was a day of relief and joy for the Bills, thrilled about seeing their fallen teammate again. Then came the opening kickoff.

Buffalo's Nyheim Hines caught the ball on his own 4-yard line. He then cut to his right, and had open space almost immediately. Hines outran two possible tacklers, and was all alone with 25 yards to go. Jim Nantz said on the CBS broadcast, "This is storybook!" Hines ran into the end zone and then hopped up to the top of the wall to take in the explosion of noise in the building. It was one of those rare moments at a sporting event where the emotions encompassed more than a game itself.

"I was running down the sideline, I looked over

and saw nobody, and I was like, 'Oh wow, I might really be gone here," Hines said. "I'm so thankful it was me to, you know, bring that juice, but it's way bigger than me and that's what I always thought about and that's what I felt all day. . . . [It was] bigger than those 10 guys today who did a great job blocking for me."

"You want the truth, it was spiritual, it really was. Bone chilling. It was special," quarterback Josh Allen said. "I can't remember a play that touched me like that, I don't think in my life. So, it's probably No. 1."

Now came the tough part—playing the rest of the game after experiencing one of the most emotional moments in the history of the stadium. Even though the Patriots weren't as good as they were during the Tom Brady days, a Bill Belichick–coached team wasn't likely to roll over . . . and it didn't. The teams traded scores, and in the third quarter, the Patriots pulled ahead. It was easy to wonder if Buffalo had run out of emotion.

Then Hines caught the ensuing kickoff 1 yard deep in the end zone. He ran up the middle, broke a tackle, and cut to the left. All of a sudden, Hines was completely alone without an opposing jersey in sight—and he still had 50 more yards to run. He covered the distance easily enough, and the Bills had the lead back.

"We've always known he's [Hines] a special returner but that was a career game for him and it couldn't have happened for us as a team at a better time," center Mitch Morse said.

Suitably inspired, the Bills pulled away from there to win the game comfortably. That last score allowed everyone connected to the team to have extra time to decompress from a memorable afternoon. The playoff implications of the day almost

BOX SCORE

	1st	2nd	3rd	4th	Final
NEW ENGLAND (L, 8-9)	7	7	3	6	23
BUFFALO (W, 13-3)	7	7	14	7	35

SCORING SUMMARY:

QTR	TEAM	PLAY
1st	BUF.	Hines 96-yard kickoff return (Bass kick)
1st	N.E.	Jones 2-yard pass to Meyers (Folk kick)
2nd	BUF.	Allen 4-yard pass to Knox (Bass kick)
2nd	N.E.	Jones 2-yard pass to Parker (Folk kick)
3rd	N.E.	Folk 24-yard field goal
3rd	BUF.	Hines 101-yard kickoff return (Bass kick)
3rd	BUF.	Allen 42-yard pass to Brown (Bass kick)
4th	N.E.	Jones 26-yard pass to Parker (pass failed)
4th	BUF.	Allen 49-yard pass to Diggs (Bass kick)

ATTENDANCE: 70,753

Nyheim Hines's opening kickoff return will never be forgotten by Bills' fans.
CREDIT GETTY IMAGES

seemed irrelevant, but they were real. Buffalo finished the season with seven straight wins, and was set to play Miami in the first round of the playoffs. A win there, and the Bills would be guaranteed of staying at home for the next round of the postseason.

But Buffalo had won a bigger victory this week, and everyone knew it.

"I usually sugarcoat it and I say, 'Oh, it's just another win.' But this one was extremely special," tackle Dion Dawkins said. "It was extremely special coming into it. We understood that we just had to get the job done. And we're blessed. Three [Hamlin's uniform number] was with us, and it's a huge win."

Ranked No. 18 of 50 by the authors.

NOTEWORTHY: *Hines became the first Bills' player to return two kickoffs for touchdowns in the same game. At that point in history, only 11 NFL players had ever done it. Allen's three touchdown passes gave him 35 for the season—the third straight season he reached that number.*

JANUARY 21, 2024

CHIEFS At BILLS

THE THREE MOST important words in real estate are said to be location, location, location. Now it was time to see if those same words applied to football playoff games.

The Bills and Chiefs had become big rivals by the time this matchup in 2024 took place. Buffalo had advanced to the AFC Championship game in January 2021, only to lose to the Chiefs in Kansas City. A little less than a year later, the teams met again in the divisional round in Kansas City, and again the Chiefs won in one of the greatest playoff games in NFL history.

Now they were set to play again in 2024, and it was time for the Bills to believe in the power of the home-field advantage. This time, the teams would

be playing in Highmark Stadium. Maybe that would be enough to push Buffalo past Kansas City.

"Even though I know it's going to be hostile and there are going to be people talking trash and everything like that, I'm excited for it because it's one of the best environments in football," Chiefs quarterback Patrick Mahomes said before the game, which was the first road playoff contest of his career.

"We understand that every time that we play them it's an all-or-nothing game and it's going to come down to us at some point during the football seasons," Bills offensive lineman Dion Dawkins said. "And they have shown in many ways that they are great, as well as us. Just be ready for a gritty, gritty football game."

Dawkins wasn't kidding. As usual the Chiefs and Bills went right down to the last couple of minutes.

The back-and-forth contest started slowly, as the Bills and Chiefs each posted a field goal in the first quarter. Early in the next period, Josh Allen ran for a score to put Buffalo ahead. Kansas City answered with a second field goal and a touchdown pass from Mahomes to Travis Kelce—a combination that was starting to live in infamy in Western New York. Allen did put the Bills ahead at the half with his second short scoring run.

Tyler Bass's missed field goal gave the Chiefs a reason to celebrate a playoff victory.
CREDIT GETTY IMAGES

The Mahomes-to-Kelce combination worked again early in the third quarter to give Kansas City a 20–17 lead. Buffalo needed about 11 minutes to retake the lead, as Allen did the throwing instead of the running this time. He hit Khalil Shakir for a score. But Isiah Pacheco of the Chiefs answered only 40 seconds into the fourth quarter to give his team a 27–24 lead.

The Bills didn't have a first down in their next two possessions, one of which ended when an oddly timed faked punt went nowhere. But the Buffalo defense compensated by causing a fumble and later by forcing a punt by Kansas City. The Bills had the ball with 8:23 left, 80 yards from the goal line with a chance to bury some ghosts. Buffalo moved the ball methodically down the field, but the drive stopped on the Kansas City 26 after two pass incompletions. At least the Bills were in field-goal range with a chance to tie.

However, there was reason for the Bills to be less than confident. Tyler Bass had been a little shaky in his kicks in recent weeks, and winds could be gusty in Orchard Park. Bass's 44-yard kick went wide right, bringing back memories of a similar Bills' miss at the end of Super Bowl XXV. From there, Kansas City picked up a needed first down on a run by Pacheco, and ran the so-called "victory formation" three times to earn the 27–24 victory.

"It's completely on me," Bass said. "I've got to do a better job of playing it a little more left when you have a left to right [wind], I've been here long enough to know you have to do that. I was trusting my line that I had in warmups. Hit a good ball, but it didn't work out. I feel terrible, you know? I love this team and it hurts. This one hurts bad."

The asterisk to the miss is a reminder that even if Bass had tied the score, the Chiefs would have had the ball with a little less than two minutes to play. Stopping Mahomes, one of the clutchest players of his generation, would have been a difficult task for the Bills. As it was, this still was exactly the type of game that everyone had predicted.

As usual, both offenses moved the ball effectively for the most part, and the outcome wasn't assured until the final few moments. Bills safety Jordan Poyer summed it up nicely when he said, "Ultimately, they made one more play than us."

So much for location, location, location. It was more of a case of frustration, frustration, frustration.

"Every season, if you don't win, it's a failed season," Allen said. "That's the nature of this business."

Ranked No. 30 of 50 by the authors.

BOX SCORE

	1ST	2ND	3RD	4TH	FINAL
KANSAS CITY (W)	3	10	7	7	27
BUFFALO (L)	3	14	7	0	24

SCORING SUMMARY:

QTR	TEAM	PLAY
1ST	BUF.	Bass 27-yard field goal
1ST	K.C.	Butker 47-yard field goal
2ND	BUF.	Allen 5-yard run (Bass kick)
2ND	K.C.	Butker 29-yard field goal
2ND	K.C.	Mahomes 22-yard pass to Kelce (Butker kick)
2ND	BUF.	Allen 2-yard run (Bass kick)
3RD	K.C.	Mahomes 3-yard from to Kelce (Butker kick)
3RD	BUF.	Allen 13-yard pass to Shakir (Bass kick)
4TH	K.C.	Pacheco 4-yard run (Butker kick)

ATTENDANCE: 70,808

NOTEWORTHY: *It was the sixth straight time the Chiefs had reached the AFC championship game. The total yardage numbers were very similar—368 for the Bills, 361 for the Chiefs. Buffalo finished with 182 yards rushing, with Allen leading the way with 72 yards on 12 carries.*

NOVEMBER 3, 2024

DOLPHINS At BILLS

DURING THE first half of the 2020s, games between the Bills and the Miami Dolphins often helped determine supremacy in the AFC East.

This matchup was not one of them. Buffalo already had a three-and-a-half game lead on the Dolphins at the midpoint of the season. The two division foes had met earlier in the season in Miami when Buffalo had dominated the Dolphins in a 31–10 victory. Almost worse than the outcome of the game for Miami was that they also lost the services of starting quarterback Tua Tagovailoa to yet another concussion. The Dolphins went into a tailspin and lost three of four games without their quarterback.

Tua had returned for the last of those games, a 28–27 loss to Arizona. But at least the Dolphins offense had been better under Tagovailoa. "It feels good to be able to come back and play with my teammates to hopefully help in any way I can get a spark going for us offensively," he said. "It was good [last week], but tough loss against a really good team."

With a 2–5 record, Miami was playing to save its season when it came to Buffalo. Buffalo, on the other hand, was looking to continue its quest for a fifth straight division title and possibly home-field advantage in the playoffs.

While a 6–2 start was quite satisfactory, it was easy to wonder if the Bills' kicking game was operating at peak efficiency. Tyler Bass had missed a game-tying field goal attempt in a home playoff loss to Kansas City in the previous season, and he hadn't been overly sharp in 2024.

Close games often come down to last-minute kicks, and Bass had something to prove at this stage in his career.

After a slow start, the two teams traded first-quarter field goals. Early in the second quarter Buffalo moved the ball well but Josh Allen was intercepted by Dolphins' cornerback Jalen Ramsey at the 3-yard line to end that threat. Miami promptly marched 97 yards in 14 plays to take the lead on a Tagovailoa to De'Von Achane touchdown pass.

Allen had the Bills on the move again before the end of the first half, but his 21-yard touchdown run was called back on a holding penalty. Buffalo settled for a field goal. The teams went to the halftime break with Miami in the lead 10–6.

Early in the third quarter Bills defensive back Taron Johnson forced a Raheem Mostert fumble that Kaiir Elam recovered for Buffalo at its 36-yard line. Allen eventually turned that Miami miscue into a 1-yard touchdown pass to Mack Hollins.

But Bass missed the extra point as boos rained down from the stands on the kicker.

Miami took the lead back on Jason Sanders's short field goal, but the Bills offense answered two plays later with a 63-yard touchdown pass from Allen to Ray Davis. "The biggest thing as a running back once you get to the third level, gotta be able to make a guy miss," Davis said. "After that, I just kind of blacked out from there." A successful two-point conversion pass from Allen to rookie Keon Coleman put Buffalo back in front 20–13.

The back-and-forth affair continued throughout the final quarter. Miami scored early in the quarter on Achane's run; Buffalo answered with a touchdown pass to Quintin Morris. Miami responded with another lengthy drive that ended with a Tagovailoa to Jason Waddle touchdown pass. The game was tied again, 27–27, with only 1:38 remaining in regulation time.

Buffalo struggled to move the ball, but penalties helped the team reach the Miami 43-yard line with 10 seconds left. Bills head coach Sean McDermott sent Bass out to attempt a 61-yard field goal. What was the likelihood that a struggling kicker could make the longest game-winning field goal in team history? But that was exactly what Bass did.

"So proud of him. So happy for him," Allen said. "Got emotional in my little postgame speech out there—just the trials and tribulations that he's been through this year . . . A 61-yard field goal to win a game against a division rival, it's what stories are made of."

"It means everything," Bass said of the kick. "Very emotional. Haven't really processed it yet, but just putting in a lot of work, man, and was just focused on right here, right now, the present and being patient with everything, man. . . . Just reminding myself that, you know, I love this, I love the sport. This is what I've dreamed of."

Ranked No. 49 of 50 by the authors.

A 61-yard field goal by Tyler Bass beat the Dolphins and set a team record for longest such kick.
CREDIT GETTY IMAGES

BOX SCORE

	1ST	2ND	3RD	4TH	FINAL
MIAMI (L, 2-6)	3	7	3	14	27
BUFFALO (W, 7-2)	3	3	14	10	30

SCORING SUMMARY:

QTR	TEAM	PLAY
1ST	BUF.	Bass 40-yard field goal
1ST	MIA.	Sanders 39-yard field goal
2ND	MIA.	Tagovailoa 14-yard pass to Achane (Sanders kick)
2ND	BUF.	Bass 49-yard field goal
3RD	BUF.	Allen 1-yard pass to Hollins (Bass kick)
3RD	MIA.	Sanders 23-yard field goal
3RD	BUF.	Allen 63-yard pass to Davis (Sanders kick)
4TH	MIA.	Achane 8-yard run (Sanders kick)
4TH	BUF.	Allen 2-yard pass to Morris (Bass kick)
4TH	MIA.	Tagovailoa 7-yard pass to Waddle (Sanders kick)
4TH	BUF.	Bass 61-yard field goal

ATTENDANCE: 70,862

NOTEWORTHY: *Allen completed 25 of 39 passes for 235 yards, three touchdowns and one interception. Buffalo's leading rusher was James Cook with only 44 yards on 10 carries as the Dolphins held the Bills to only 94 yards rushing. Buffalo had eight players that caught passes from Allen. "That is our team—everybody eats," Hollins said. "Like we'll eat off the floor if we have to. It is what it is. Like we don't care. We're just trying to get something to eat. We're hungry. Every game we're hungry."*

ONE BILLS DRIVE

NOVEMBER 17, 2024

CHIEFS At BILLS

BY 2024, games between the Bills and Chiefs had become the most anticipated matchup of the season—particularly in the two cities involved. They had been playing memorable games for a few years by then, and they featured two of the league's most exciting and best quarterbacks in Kansas City's Patrick Mahomes and Buffalo's Josh Allen.

They had met seven times before this, and Mahomes had a narrow 4–3 margin in wins. The "rivalry" reminded people of when Tom Brady of the Patriots and Peyton Manning of the Colts always seemed to be in each other's way during the course of great seasons.

"You're playing the best of the best," Mahomes said of Allen to *The Buffalo News*. "That's what you want in this league."

While this meeting didn't have the extra juice that a playoff game could provide, it did have a nice little twist. The Chiefs came into the game with a perfect 9–0 record, while the Bills were 8–2. The football world wondered if Buffalo could end Kansas City's streak of 15 straight wins over two seasons . . . and provide some excitement along the way.

That's exactly what happened. As a bonus, Allen delivered a moment in the clutch that will be remembered for years.

The game had its first dramatic moment on the second play from scrimmage. Taylor Rapp intercepted Mahomes' pass to Juju Smith-Schuster, and the Bills capitalized to quickly score the game's first points. But the Chiefs answered with a score of their own to go up by 7–6.

More scores were traded in the second quarter, and Tyler Bass's field goal at the gun lifted Buffalo to a 16–14 halftime lead. Neither team scored in the third quarter, but

Josh Allen's winning touchdown run was a magical moment in franchise history.
CREDIT GETTY IMAGES

in the fourth quarter Allen found Curtis Samuel for a score to give Buffalo a nine-point lead at 23–14. Still, with 12:51 to play, no one thought that margin was safe.

Sure enough, Mahomes responded with a touchdown pass to Noah Gray with a little under eight minutes left. Now the Bills needed a nice long drive to kill some time and take a bigger lead. After running 11 plays, they had the ball on fourth down and two on the Chiefs' 26. Time for a field goal?

No. That would have given Mahomes about two minutes to try to score a go-ahead touchdown. Instead, the Bills coaches gave the ball to Allen, who took off on a delayed run. About six players on the Kansas City defense missed the Buffalo quarterback on his way to the end zone. CBS announcer Jim Nantz yelled at the end of the play, "Oh, the play of the year in the NFL!"

"When Josh takes off, I find myself just watching, like, 'Wow, he's different,'" wide receiver Khalil Shakir said. "When he took off today, I just started yelling. I couldn't stop yelling. I was blanking in the head."

Not only did the play wrap up the 30–21 win, it was instantly recognized as the defining moment in Allen's pro career to that point.

"I appreciated coach for trusting us," Allen said after the game. "Any time you give the ball back to Pat [Mahomes], that offense, down six with the game on the line, I like their odds in that situation. So wanting six or seven [points] to try to make it a two-score game."

Mahomes added, "That was a guy making a play in the big moment. "Whenever the play is not there, he does a great job of making plays happen. And that's what he did on that last play."

The Chiefs did have time for one last gasp in the final moments. However, the Bills—who had intercepted Mahomes' first pass of the day—grabbed his last to make it a symmetrical finish. This one belonged to linebacker Terrel Bernard.

"Incredible play," Rapp said about the work of his teammate. "It kind of brought me back to his Houston interception—roaming back on it, a great-hands catch. To end a game like that, it was a huge, huge play."

On the Kansas City side, it was the Chiefs' first loss in 328 days. They saw their hopes for becoming the first team in 51 yards to go undefeated through the Super Bowl (Miami, 1973) go by the boards. After the game, they weren't too concerned about losing for the first time. "It's a great game to learn from for some of our young guys. Two good teams play each other, the margin between winning and losing is small," Kansas City coach Andy Reid said. "We can all learn from it and take something out of it to make us better down the road there. And we'll do that."

"The undefeated thing was cool, but that's not our ultimate goal," Mahomes said.

Ranked No. 8 of 50 by the authors.

BOX SCORE

	1ST	2ND	3RD	4TH	FINAL
KANSAS CITY (L, 9-1)	0	14	0	7	21
BUFFALO (W, 9-2)	6	10	0	14	30

SCORING SUMMARY:

QTR	TEAM	PLAY
1ST	BUF.	Cook 3-yard run (kick failed)
2ND	K.C.	Mahomes 10-yard pass to Worthy (Shrader kick)
2ND	BUF.	Cook 6-yard run (Bass kick)
2ND	K.C.	Mahomes 2-yard pass to Gray (Shrader kick)
2ND	BUF.	Bass 33-yard field goal
4TH	BUF.	Allen 12-yard pass to Samuel (Bass kick)
4TH	K.C.	Mahomes 1-yard pass to Gray (Shrader kick)
4TH	BUF.	Allen 26-yard run (Bass kick)

ATTENDANCE: 71,112

NOTEWORTHY: *Allen was 27 of 40 for 262 passing yards, and reached 25,000 passing yards for his career. He also passed O.J. Simpson for second place in the Bills' record book for rushing touchdowns, only trailing Thurman Thomas.*

JANUARY 19, 2025

RAVENS At BILLS

HERE'S A GAME that's all about star power. When the Bills hosted the Baltimore Ravens in the AFC Divisional Round of the NFL playoffs, the quarterbacks received most of the pregame attention. Josh Allen of the Bills and Lamar Jackson of the Ravens were considered the top two contenders for the Most Valuable Player Award in the National Football League. In a season in which the Bills were considered likely to take a step back after some salary cap purges, Allen took his game to a new level. He led Buffalo to the No. 2 seed in the AFC playoffs.

Jackson already was a two-time winner of the MVP trophy (2019 and 2023), and he also upped his game in 2024. Jackson threw 41 touchdown passes with four interceptions, and ran for 915 yards and four touchdowns. He and the Ravens won the matchup with Allen and the Bills in the regular season, but the return meeting was more meaningful and would be played in Buffalo.

"This is what fans are looking for, right?" CBS commentator and former NFL quarterback Matt Ryan told *The Buffalo News*. "This is what it's all about, watching two guys like this match up."

The game featured excellent performances from both men on a cold day that figured to leave most offenses frozen. Still, no one could have seen the surprise ending coming.

Khalil Shakir was a constant threat in the Bills' passing game, catching six passes against the Ravens.
CREDIT GETTY IMAGES

The Ravens, who had dominated play in the first matchup at home back in September, looked as if they were ready for a re-run. Baltimore effortlessly moved the ball down the field for the opening touchdown. But the Bills answered with a pair of scoring runs to take a 14–7 midway through the second quarter. Buffalo even had a good answer for Justin Tucker's second field goal, in the form of Allen's second touchdown run. The Bills had a 21–10 lead at the half, and the team's chances of advancing looked good.

Baltimore, however, had other ideas in the third quarter. After another field goal, the Ravens' powerful running back Derrick Henry rammed the ball into the end zone. The conversion failed, leaving the Bills with a mere two-point lead and 16 minutes left to play. The Bills answered with a pair of field goals to go up 27–19, capitalizing on the Ravens' self-destruction. One promising drive in the fourth quarter ended when Buffalo's Terrel Bernard stripped Baltimore tight end Mark Andrews of the ball. It was one of three Ravens' turnovers on the day, a number that often proves fatal to a team that has hopes of advancing in the playoffs.

"I think that's part of our philosophy when we first got together in the spring, is who we want to be as a defense," Bernard said about the turnovers. "That's one of the first points is stop the run and then take the ball away. . . . Our fundamentals, our execution, but then, the ball. That's the key point has been all year for us. When we're successful taking the ball away, we have a good chance to win."

Baltimore still had one last chance to tie the game in the final 3:19 of play. Jackson deftly moved his team on a drive of 88 yards, connecting with Isaiah Likely for a score. "Lamar, he be making stuff happen. I can't lie. He's good at that," Bills defensive back Rasul Douglas said.

That left the climatic two-point conversion at-

The legs of Josh Allen proved crucial in a playoff win over the Ravens.
CREDIT GETTY IMAGES

tempt. Jackson rolled right, and saw Andrews open on the right side with an apparent clear path to the end zone. But the three-time Pro Bowler couldn't catch the ball, and it fell to the ground.

From there, the Bills, once they recovered the on-side kick, only needed to run out the clock. They did so, and Buffalo had taken a difficult 27–25 win.

Ponder this statistic: The Ravens became the first team in league history to run for 175 yards, complete 70 percent of its passes, average 10 yards per pass, convert 70 percent of third downs,

BOX SCORE

	1ST	2ND	3RD	4TH	FINAL
BALTIMORE (L)	7	3	9	6	25
BUFFALO (W)	7	14	0	6	27

SCORING SUMMARY:

QTR	TEAM	PLAY
1ST	BAL.	Jackson 16-yard pass to Bateman (Tucker kick)
1ST	BUF.	Davis 1-yard run (Bass kick)
2ND	BUF.	Allen 1-yard run (Bass kick)
2ND	BAL.	Tucker 26-yard field goal
2ND	BUF.	Allen 4-yard run (Bass kick)
3RD	BAL.	Tucker 47-yard field goal
3RD	BAL.	Henry 5-yard run (pass failed)
4TH	BUF.	Bass 51-yard field goal
4TH	BUF.	Bass 21-yard field goal
4TH	BAL.	Jackson 24-yard pass to Likely (pass failed)

ATTENDANCE: 70,697

and have no punts or missed field goals . . . and lose.

"What a complete win," Allen said. "All year, this team has heard we've got no talent, we're too small, we can't stop the run, we're not good enough to compete. We've just put our head down and worked hard. I'm so proud of our defense. I'm so proud of our offense and special teams."

Andrews took some of the spotlight away from the winners because of the two plays—the fumble and the drop—in the fourth quarter.

"One play doesn't define anybody. He's the all-time leading touchdown receiver in Ravens history," safety Kyle Hamilton said. "He's been a consistent beacon of success the whole time he's been here."

Ranked No. 20 of 50 by the authors.

NOTEWORTHY: *The Bills played 10 games in Highmark Stadium that season, and won them all. The Bills also had been perfect at home in the 1988 and 1990 seasons. Jackson was 18 of 25 for 254 yards, but he threw an interception and fumbled. Allen threw for 127 yards and ran for 20 more.*

INDEX